THE VIRTUE OF
WEALTH

Advanced praise for *The Virtue of Wealth*

Paul has always impressed me as an author. His insights are beyond just the financial realm. This book takes an even broader perspective I find stimulating and calming.

—JOHN SESTINA, CFP®, CHFC, PRESIDENT OF THE SESTINA NETWORK OF
FEE-ONLY FINANCIAL PLANNING PROFESSIONALS

The Virtue of Wealth is a thought provoking, practical guide to achieving financial success in all phases of our lives. Refreshingly there is no "hype," instead clear and gentle explanations leading the reader to an understanding that true insight comes from viewing financial aspirations against the wider philosophical considerations of our lives. The book encourages the reader to think deeply about what is important for them whilst at the same time pointing out options for accepting and dealing with the reality in which we live. It contains useful tools for understanding and maintaining balance and personal financial integrity in a complex and often paradoxical world.

—ANNE O'DONNELL, MANAGING DIRECTOR, AUSTRALIAN ETHICAL INVESTMENT LTD.

Whether we realize it or not, the human tendency is to construct our lives around the idea that our doing first leads to having which in turns leads to being. With compassion and brilliance, Paul masterfully leads us on a journey of transformation to a better understanding that Being always precedes having and doing.

—SCOTT NEAL, CPA®, CFP®, MBA AND PRESIDENT OF D. SCOTT NEAL, INC.

Our culture has a love affair with money, but in this thought-provoking volume Paul Sutherland reminds us where we should look for our true wealth. With insight and clarity he shows how we can make peace with our checkbooks and lead lives of freedom and balance.

—ROGER WELLINGTON, EXECUTIVE DIRECTOR OF KINDER INSTITUTE OF LIFE PLANNING

THE VIRTUE OF
WEALTH

CREATING LIFE SUCCESS THE *Zenvesting* WAY

PAUL H. SUTHERLAND

Spirituality & Health Books

The Tao te Ching *verses are quoted from Tolbert McCarrol's translation*
(Crossroad Publishing Company, 1982).
For a full bibliography of texts used in the development of this book, see www.zenvesting.com.

· Cover Design by Barbara Hodge & Heather Shaw.
Cover art: *Handaka Sonja*; drawing on paper; ink and light colors; 27.1 x 38.8 cm.; Hokusai School;
from the Library of Congress Japanese prints and drawings collection.
To order directly from the publisher, please go online to www.spiritualityhealthbooks.com
Any other inquiries can be mailed to:
Spirituality & Health Books
129 ½ East Front Street
Traverse City MI 49686 USA

ISBN 978-0-9818708-0-9
Sutherland, Paul H.
        The virtue of wealth : creating life success the zenvesting way /
        Paul H. Sutherland.—1st ed.—Traverse City, MI : Spirituality & Health Books, c2009.
        p. ; cm.
        ISBN: 978-0-9818708-0-9
        Includes bibliographical references and index.
        1. Finance, Personal. 2. Investments. 3. Wealth. 4. Success.
        5. Zen Buddhism. I. Title.
HG4527 .S88 2009
332.6—dc22 0905

First Printing 2009
Manufactured in China

Dedicated to
Khan Abdul Ghaffar
and his
"Servants of God"

*Blessed is the person who gives advice; one thousand times more blessed
is the person who takes the advice and uses it.*

—MIDDLE EAST PROVERB

contents

Worksheets & Guides

introduction

HOW DO WE FEED OUR SOUL?

Since my early teens, I've been searching for the truth about success in any number of books including a few that continue to grace my bookshelves, *The Law of Success*, and *Think and Grow Rich* by Napoleon Hill and *The Richest Man in Babylon* by George S. Clason. Another aspect of my search involved Bible study with the Methodists, Sunday catechism at Saint Philip's, and Wednesday meetings at the Christian Science Church—all before I was out of high school.

Every year since, despite continued reading, attending lectures, and a masters in Business, I have felt the world becoming less and less clear. Fortunately, I have found that by relaxing my desire to *know*, I can make the truth seem less clouded. If I stop grasping, stop looking so hard, if I take a moment to breathe, and inspect my own nature, I often find that truth stands straight, clear and full of virtue right in front of me.

To me, life and truth are about relationships. Life and truth are about our interdependence. But *knowing* this has little practical benefit unless we express it, or, as the Bible says, we let our cup runneth over and practice it. Day to day, the practical expression of love and virtue is how we feed our soul.

What I have learned in my search for truth and success is found in this oh-so-practical "how to" book. The lessons come from unbiased observations of clients, family, friends, work associates, and other generous professionals that have shared their goals, hopes, fears, loves, disappointments, joys and common sense with me. It is their lives and experiences that have made this book possible. In other words, I believe the truth of success lies in opening up and allowing yourself to experience, contribute to, and learn from the relationships that are all around you. I hope this book encourages you to stop grasping and follow your own true nature toward truth and success.

Blessings,

Paul

chapter 1

WHAT IS HAPPINESS?

If powerful men and women could center themselves in it, the whole world would be transformed by itself, in its natural rhythms. People would be content with their simple everyday lives, in harmony, and free of desire. When there is no desire, all things are at peace.—TAO TE CHING

Better writers than myself have found it nearly impossible to communicate the subtle ways to create lasting happiness. No doubt this has to do with the not so subtle differences in opinion as to what qualifies as "lasting happiness." For some people, it may be becoming a parent. For others, it may be the weaving and palette-making of gardening. There are those who may only find true happiness while fishing, while others would rather spend their days talking to coworkers and clients. Not only are there profound variations between people, but what makes one person happy one day might not work the next: a rainy summer day is a pleasant respite, two rainy days is a waste of time.

Money alone will never be enough to make you happy. (You've been told that before, haven't you? Well, believe it.) Gregg Easterbrook in his book *The Progress Paradox*, boiled the non-starter down to simple economics: "Most of what people really want in life—love, friendship, respect, family, standing, fun—is not priced and does not pass through the market. If something isn't priced you can't buy it, so possessing money may not help much." As Lennon/ McCartney said: **Can't buy me love.**

What I do know, however, is that money, while it can't make you happy, can sure make you blue. And, while I can't tell you how to create lasting happiness, **I can tell you how to create lasting wealth.**

Talking or keeping silent, single or married, rich or poor at retirement, it's all a matter of making choices. Life is one long chain of choices, from the mundane to the monumental, and the shape of those decisions ultimately defines us. Each day we choose where, when, why, what and who we are. The responsibility is ours alone. Aristotle said, "Happiness is not a separate feeling state that can be obtained in any other way save as part and parcel to right action."

This book is written to encourage readers to recognize the wealth-related choices we make each day so that we might understand and anticipate the results. Of course, randomness and chance always play a part in our lives. We might win the lottery or the stock market might crash, but even so, it is our actions—and attitudes—that will ultimately shape our future. Life is 1% the events that we experience and 99% our attitude and decisions, whether wise or naïve.

The question is, what is it that we seek in life? I know, for me, that when I'm sick, health becomes a top priority. When I'm lonely, relationships are my desire. At leisure, creative expression comes to mind. Our true needs are simple, but because of the vast array of options available to us, we tend to forget this. Often we equate the pleasure of buying more, bigger, expensive goods such as homes, cars, boats and TVs with happiness. These things may certainly infuse us with momentary excitement but they will not bring us lasting fulfillment.

Most of us briefly studied the work of Ralph Waldo Emerson in high school English classes. I bring up Emerson because, after all his life experience—being raised by a Unitarian minister, attending Harvard University at fourteen, losing first, his one true love, and then his son— after years of intellectual partnership and sparring with the likes of Henry David Thoreau and Nathanial Hawthorne, drawing both huge crowds and financial success with his stimulating lectures and complex books of essays, he remained convinced that a man's needs really are simple.

One of those needs, perhaps the most vital, is forming close relationships with family and friends—relationships based on internal and not external factors.

What does that mean?

External factors are the choices we make that show what kind of person we are. The house we live in, the car we drive and the purse we carry all make a statement about the kind of person we are inside. The internal factors are the feelings about ourselves, and others, that influence these decisions.

HAPPINESS DEPENDS

UPON OURSELVES.

—ARISTOTLE

HE WHO LOVES THE

WORLD AS HIS BODY

MAY BE ENTRUSTED

WITH THE EMPIRE.

—TAO TE CHING

We need to ask ourselves: will our neighbors **really** ignore us if there is not a brand new car in our driveway? If we aren't wearing the right clothes, will our friends **really** abandon us? Will we feel diminished if we have no flat screen TV, or, heaven forbid, own only a single TV? And if these neighbors and friends are the people we are trying to please, what does that say about our inner life? No wonder we feel lonely.

Imagine what life would be like if in every household, each family agreed about what they would watch together on television instead of retreating to different rooms and watching their favorite show all by themselves. Indeed, imagine if in every household family members agreed that they would prefer to talk, take a walk or play a board game rather than turn on the TV. Imagine what life would be like if the ability to walk next door on a warm evening and chat was the basis of neighborly friendship, instead of the sticker price of that shiny car. Imagine the fun of laughing with a friend, instead of judging them for wearing the wrong brand of pants.

While the external part of us might think that being richer, more beautiful, having a different spouse, a better job or different parents is the key to making our lives come together to create happiness; internally, we know this is non-sense. Great relationships, safety, health, security, creative expression, spiritual renewal, time to savor life and personal fulfillment have less to do with money and good looks and more to do with attitude and choice.

Think again about what Aristotle said: "Happiness is not a separate feeling state that can be obtained in any other way save as part and parcel to right action."

The Middle Way

The Buddha does not want us to follow the double path—desire and indulgence on the one hand and fear and aversion on the other. Just be aware of pleasure, he teaches. Anger, fear, dissatisfaction are not the path of the yogi but the path of worldly people. The tranquil person walks the Middle Path of right practice, leaving grasping on the left and fear and aversion on the right.

One who undertakes the path of practice must follow this Middle Way: "I will not take interest in pleasure or pain. I will lay them down." But, of course, it is hard at first. It is as though we are being kicked on both sides. Like a cowbell or a pendulum, we are knocked back and forth.

When Buddha preached his first sermon, he discoursed on these two extremes because this is where attachment lies. The desire for happiness kicks from the one side; suffering and dissatisfaction kick from the other. These two nemeses are always besieging us. But when you walk the Middle Path, you put them both down.

Don't you see? If you follow these extremes, you will simply strike out when you are angry and grab for what attracts you, without the slightest patience or forbearance. How long can you go on being trapped in this way? Consider it: if you like something, you follow after it when liking arises, yet it is just drawing you on to seek suffering. This mind of desire is really clever. Where will it lead you next?

The Buddha teaches us to keep laying down the extremes. This is the path of right practice, the path leading out of birth and becoming. On this path, there is neither pleasure nor pain, neither good nor evil. Alas, the mass of humans filled with desiring just strive for pleasure and always bypass the middle, missing the Path of the Excellent One, the path of the seeker of truth. Attached to birth and becoming, happiness and suffering, good and evil, the one who does not travel this Middle Path cannot become a wise one, cannot find liberation. Our Path is straight, the path of tranquility and pure awareness, calmed of both elation and sorrow. If your heart is like this, you can stop asking other people for guidance.

You will see that when the heart/mind is unattached, it is abiding in its normal state. When it stirs from the normal because of various thoughts and feelings, the process of thought construction takes place, in which illusions are created. Learn to see through this process. When the mind has stirred from normal, it leads away from right practice to one of the extremes of indulgence or aversion, thereby creating more illusion, more thought construction. Good or bad only arises in your mind. If you keep a watch on your mind, studying this one topic your whole life, I guarantee that you will never be bored.

The truth is, we can have happiness. Consciously believing the truth of that statement is the first step to manifesting the unique vision we all have for our lives.

Visualization is a powerful tool not because of the images you create, but because of the values and feelings you inadvertently inhabit while constructing the thoughts or images. Things and images have only temporal and representative meaning. Values are universal, eternal and charged with momentum for manifestation.

—ELIA WISE, *LETTER TO EARTH*

Visioning Worksheet

What is your vision for life? What do you want your tomorrows to look like? As you close your eyes and consider these questions, your ideas will coalesce into a tangible philosophy that is based on your values.

The following desires are easy to place in a vision statement:

I/we want financial security.

I/we want to live in a nice house.

I/we want our children to be in good schools.

I/we want to have a healthy, balanced lifestyle.

I/we want time to enjoy our children.

I/we want to enjoy our careers.

I/we want a big, wonderful life outside our careers.

I/we want to use part of our talents to help others.

I/we want to be able to retire someday without financial worries.

I/we want to take a walk each day.

I/we want to take piano lessons.

I/we want to express our talents helping people in the developing world.

Now, what do you most care about?

Who do you care about?

What do you most want to do?

I am a prisoner of hope. I'm going to die full of hope. There's no doubt about that, because that is a choice I make.—CORNEL WEST

The idea that we have a genetic "set point" of happiness from which we hardly deviate is no longer considered the whole story. There's pretty convincing evidence that we can retrain our brains and emotions to a far greater degree than was thought. True, some people are just naturally sunny. But for many of us, happiness is a decision. We set an intention to be happy, then follow up with conscious effort, such as reframing negative thinking and becoming more flexible… Happiness is a posture toward life.
—DANIEL NETTLE, *HAPPINESS: THE SCIENCE BEHIND YOUR SMILE*

chapter 2

TRADING TIME FOR MONEY

Don't tell me you will love me forever.
Tell me that you will love me
Thursday afternoon at four o'clock. —W. H. AUDEN

SOCIETY, THE MEDIA, OUR FRIENDS AND FAMILY all directly or indirectly contribute to a culture of getting and spending. **Wants** can feel like **needs** when the neighbors have **one**, your kids want **one**, and your mother asks why you don't have **one**. But we pay a dear price for looking trendy, getting it now and getting it quick. A short attention span is expensive and consumes time. Are we missing out on life by using precious time to shop for, buy, store and take care of our stuff? Getting and spending has taken the place of earning, relaxing, enjoying life and saving.

*I love to travel. Every five days, I move. I don't mind if it's not glamorous.
I travel lighter than anyone I know. I am a great packer. It's always the
same: some dresses, a coat, pants, evening top, a few T-shirts. The only
heavy things are my vitamins and my hiking boots. I always say, 'If you can
figure out your suitcase, you can figure out life.'*—DIANE VON FURSTENBERG

Stuff.

"Why do we have it, where do we get it and why do we keep accumulating
more of it?" MSN financial writer M.P. Dunleavey wants to know. More practically,
what is it costing us, not just in storage space and maintenance, but in time; time
lost as we dream, plan, and obsess about stuff. Perhaps we should think of our
stuff as a verb; used this way, the word stuff means, "cram, fill, plug, block, gorge."
See "Gluttony," according to *Roget's Thesaurus*.

How do we step off this **work/buy** treadmill? First, connect with the fact that
we trade time for money. If I make $18 an hour and buy a shirt for $50, I've just
spent three hours working for a shirt. Three hours away from those I love, three
hours away from yoga, a good book, reading to my kids, chatting on the phone with
a friends or teaching English as a second language. We trade money for time!

Now ask yourself, in a non-judgmental way, "What else could I do with the
money?" For example, you could buy yourself a little closer to retirement, pay
for a tutor for your kids, put it toward a down payment on a home or pay off an
old debt. You could send it to an organization that helps some of the two billion
people in the world who sleep on dirt, eat one meal a day if they're lucky, walk
hours for water and know that if they get hurt or sick, they'll likely die.

Money and time. We're back to the question of choices. We make a choice every time we spend money: it ultimately defines us. How we spend our money and our time reveals to the world and ourselves what we truly believe in.

Toyota Prius—starting at $22,000 ....Monthly cost: $433
BMW SUV—starting at $38,000..Monthly cost: $746

Banana Republic Leather Handbag...$240
Prada Leather Handbag..$2000

Coach fare ticket to Beijing (from NYC) $845
First Class ticket to Beijing (from NYC)..$12,000

Income: $35,000/yr = $17/hr
            $50,000/yr = $24/hr
            $75,000/yr = $36/hr
            $100,000/yr = $48/hr

Income/yr	Toyota Prius (total vs monthly pmts)	BMW SUV (total vs monthly pmts)	Banana Republic Bag	Prada Bag	Coach to Beijing	First Class to Beijing
$35,000	1294/25 hrs	2235/44	14	118	50	706
$50,000	916/18	1583/31	10	83	35	500
$75,000	611/12	1056/21	7	56	23	333
$100,000	458/9	792/16	5	42	18	250

Rationalizing Wealth

I promised myself I'd rarely use statistics in this book. Why? Because I believe that we are all individuals and we need to live by our own values and rhythm. If I say that the average American watches forty hours of TV a week, you might say, "Gosh, I'm not so bad. I only watch thirty-eight." If I say the average American produces four and a half pounds of trash a day, you can say, "Well, I'm about average, no big deal."

Using this logic, you can rationalize anything, no matter how extreme. In some cultures, it is alright to rape a woman as punishment for her brother's adultery. In some cultures, young girls' genitalia are mutilated as a passage to womanhood. In some cultures, it is acceptable to buy oil from the country that turns out almost half of the world's suicide bombers. The best we can do is act according to our highest "utopian" right; everything else is insincere. Comparing ourselves to others in order to justify immoral or unkind behavior should feel equally unsatisfying.

At some point in our maturity most of us forgo the need to attach a carrot to our acts of benevolence, for all around us there are reminders of the benefits of kindness and upstanding behavior. **Actions have consequences. Jesus said, "Whatsoever a man soweth, that shall he reap."** Hindu culture stresses that kindness and honesty are their own rewards. In fact, all religions acknowledge the strain caused by unseemly behavior. Our actions should be consistent with what is right and in harmony with our needs.

Kindness—of all the virtues, that's the most important.
That makes me feel optimistic about the world.—DAVE MATTHEWS

Kindness in words creates confidence. Kindness in thinking creates
profoundness. Kindness in giving creates love.—TAO TE CHING

Our ability to rationalize is one of the traits that make us human, but to err is human too. My father died when he was only fifty-three, leaving my mom with four of my five siblings still at home. Dad had been "Mr. Sutherland, the elementary school principal" to thousands of kids and dozens of teachers at a rural school in northern Michigan. He was also a smoker—Winston cigarettes for twenty years until the FDA warning labels said to stop, and even then, he continued to smoke a pipe. In the end, he died of cancer and his death touched a great many people. **For any of us to assume that we are the only ones affected by our behavior is perhaps the most selfish of rationalizations.** My dad's smoking not only left his six children fatherless, but also left my children without a Grandpa Dale and his teachers without a mentor.

Don't live in the Victim-hood

Fame or integrity: which is more important?

Money or happiness: which is more valuable?

Success or failure: which is more destructive?

If you look to others for fulfillment,
you will never truly be fulfilled.

If your happiness depends on money,
you will never be happy with yourself.

Be content with what you have; rejoice in the ways things are.
When you realize there is nothing lacking, the whole world belongs to you.

—TAO TE CHING

Abundant is the adjective to describe the amount of literature available on learned dependence and accumulation disorders. The same thing can be said for therapists and friends who tell you, "It's not your fault," or "You're a victim." Listen, if you enjoy being a victim, this book will not help you. Save it for your next life or give it to a friend who believes in pulling the arrows out of his body. Victims prefer to leave the arrow there to fester, relishing the sympathy.

Anyone who has the privilege of carrying a United States passport (or a passport from any other developed country) and who complains about his or her personal circumstances, needs to find new friends who care enough to say, "Shut up and quit feeling sorry for yourself. **You are one of the luckiest people in the world and, at least around me, please pretend to be happy!"**

They also need to re-read Einstein on relativity. Einstein wrote and taught about relativity and the truths of space and time. Had he been a psychologist, I think he would have written books with titles like, *Envy and Relativity: Why Comparing our Lives to Others is Not Helpful,* or *I Was Sad Because I had No Shoes and Then I Met a Man with No Feet.*

It's relative!

Listen to Einstein. Be aware of your place on the continuum of human experience and your good luck in being born where you were.

Once you know what you really want...

Years ago, I asked my father why he didn't aspire to be superintendent of schools, a job with a much higher pay than his principal's salary. He had been offered the position, he acknowledged, but turned it down because he was reluctant to spend more time involved in school politics and evening meetings. He admitted to being a hopeless family man and hugged me, scratching his scruffy face against mine.

As you might imagine, my parent's realistic family budget included used cars and a home completed by the labor of six kids managing paintbrushes and hammers. There was no extra money to fund college accounts or to pay for family vacations, and hand-me-down clothing was the norm.

The tradeoff my parents made was to move to Glen Arbor, a village in northern Michigan near the Sleeping Bear Dunes National Park, so we would have access to lakes, forests and outdoor activities. When we grew to be teenagers, we lived in the perfect spot to take on summer jobs at farms and seasonal restaurants. Looking back, I cannot imagine a better environment to have been raised in.

Gentle Budgeting

We need to know what we want in order to make good decisions about what to acquire and what to let go. If we want health, we need to let go of cigarettes and unhealthy foods, and we need to embrace exercise and movement. Healthy finances also come from acting on our desires with mindfulness and purpose. Gentle Budgeting is a good first step on the path towards achieving healthy financial goals.

I think most people fall into a good pattern of budgeting eventually. I do, however, believe in being realistic, being conscious of over-spending and forecasting expenses and income into the future—especially before I ever buy a home, give significant sums to friends, kids or to charity, set aside money for retirement and college or plan my vacations.

I also know some people are not good at budgeting or living within their means. So if you want to do this budgeting thing, there are three important steps, and they require patience and thoughtfulness.

First, read all of *The Virtue of Wealth*. Don't fill out the budget sheets now. Wait. Read this book to the end and then fill them out. After a few months of monitoring your desires, needs, thoughts about money, budgeting and, of course, your expenses, you will have a better understanding of the flow of money in your life.

Then, over the next three months, without judgment, project your expenses and savings in the white column of the Gentle Budgeting Worksheet.

At the end of the first month, fill in the green column with the real amount of your expenditures. Do this for three months.

Have fun, but realize you trade time for money. Eventually you'll find your ideal budget, the one that matches your lifetime goals and commitments, and the one you're going to work toward.

If the idea of budgeting scares you, then you're allowing victimhood rather than responsibility and realism to guide you.

You can do this!

You are not a victim of low income or overspending.

If you're broke or fall short each month, then you've made bad choices.

They can be fixed. **You can do this!**

See the Gentle Budgeting Worksheet on page 183 or download a larger version at www.zenvesting.com

A Moment with Zen Master Wu Bong

One thing that is not always clear to us as we go through our daily routine is that if we look at our life, if we think about it and try to analyze it, we find that there are not so many 'important' events—events that have great significance, great meaning. Mostly our life, moment by moment, is composed of very mundane tasks, very small things...

I like to tell the story of how an avalanche comes to take place. If we start to trace the cause of an avalanche, we find that often it's a very minute action. Maybe somebody speaks too loudly and that loosens a small rock and that rock loosens a bigger rock, and so on and so on. Just one small thing that is very insignificant, through a chain of events, comes to be very meaningful and has a big impact.

In a way, it is the same with our practice. We don't often realize the power of practice. One day, one retreat, just coming here on this Sunday morning and doing what we're doing. What kind of significance will it have? We don't understand right now. What Zen teaches us is not to make those distinctions about whether something is important or not important. But as we go, moment by moment, we are asked to pay attention—to give ourselves fully to this moment, one hundred percent. It doesn't matter whether it is an important moment or not an important moment; it is the only moment we have.

So what I emphasize is that in fact the only thing, the only true thing that we ever have is this moment. The past we cannot touch. The future we cannot grasp. And if we try to catch the present, it's already gone.

Excerpted from a talk at the start of the One Day Retreat on Sunday, June 17, 1990, Providence Zen Center. (www.providencezen.org)

chapter 3

ACHIEVING INDEPENDENCE

If you don't live it,
it won't come out of your horn.—CHARLIE PARKER

The reality is that young relationships often catch the brunt of financial anxiety: incomes are lower, savings are often non-existent and household expenditures are ever present. Incorporating restraint and long-term thinking, humor, understanding, acceptance and diplomacy into the cauldron of new love can be a difficult task. Thoughts of savings and budgets are the last thing our mind wants to contemplate, but whether you are single or married, partnered or living in a communal system, this money thing must be mastered. Let's take it slowly…

As a group, Americans are spenders, not savers. This has been especially evident in our financial behavior since 1982. Back then the average savings rate was 11.2%, according to the Investment Company Institute (ICI). In 2008, it was less than zero—and just when the Baby Boomers are in their peak earning years, too.

What makes this negative savings rate so distressing is that those same Baby Boomers are ramping up for a mass exodus from the workforce over the next two decades as they begin to retire. Twelve thousand Americans will turn sixty each day for the next eighteen years. Their retirements will most likely include longer life spans, higher health care costs and in many instances, a negligible pension.

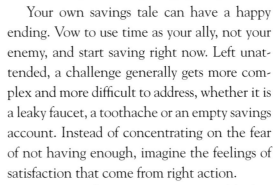

Your own savings tale can have a happy ending. Vow to use time as your ally, not your enemy, and start saving right now. Left unattended, a challenge generally gets more complex and more difficult to address, whether it is a leaky faucet, a toothache or an empty savings account. Instead of concentrating on the fear of not having enough, imagine the feelings of satisfaction that come from right action.

Saving is the surest way to wealth, but rationalization can get in our way. We can always come up with a reason not to save. Instead, do it now! Go grab a piece of paper and write down all of the reasons you cannot save—every one of them!

REASONS NOT TO SAVE

1. I/we don't make enough money as it is.

2. I/we have too much debt.

3.

4.

5.

6.

7.

8.

9.

10.

Before marriage and before kids are great times when saving lots is easier. Sadly, while the young may have lots of discretionary income, the attitude often is, "Why save? Life is long!" **Beware: Stuff happens.** Sooner or later.

Don't let time become your enemy. Don't let the idea of a new baby, an anniversary, vacation, or (heaven forbid) retirement catch you with a hollow nest egg.

You can do it!

Think about some important reasons to save.
    Now, write them down.

REASONS TO SAVE

1.

2.

3.

4.

5.

Never stand begging for what you have the power to earn.

—MIGUEL DE CERVANTES

Done with your list? What do you see there? Vacation? Illness? Baby? Boat?

Money is security in our society. But it's also control, the freedom to make our own choices. A big investment or savings account can pay our hospital bills, support us if we lose our job and fund both our education and our retirement. To not save and build up a nest egg is as foolish as believing that the sun will set in the east tomorrow night. Never, ever forget: **Stuff happens!** When it does, money helps to clean up the mess. Legal bills, home help and time off from work during my divorce were all paid for from savings. Divorce hits half of us, disability before age sixty-five hits half of us, and changing jobs or being jobless for a while will happen to almost every one of us.

Look at your list again, and figure out how to save 10% of your paycheck each month.

Write it down.

How It Could Work For a Young Couple

Let's take Dale, age twenty-four, who is in his first job and earns $28,000.

Dale participates fully in the 401(k) at work, saving $500 monthly with his company matching an additional $250 for a total monthly savings of $750.

By the age of twenty-seven, assuming a rate of return of 7%, he has saved $29,947.58 in his 401(k) plan.

But, at age twenty-seven, he gets engaged and decides to reduce his 401(k) contribution to save for his wedding and a down payment on a home. Dale reduces his contribution to $100 a month, with his company matching an additional $50 for a total of $150 a month. This continues for the next year, allowing Dale's 401(k) savings to grow to $33,971.38.

After one year Dale marries Carrie, twenty-four, who teaches and makes $33,000. Dale is now earning $33,000, as well. Both are committed to saving 10% of their income towards retirement. Carrie saves $275 a month in a 403(b) plan and Dale saves $275 though his 401(k), with his company matching $137.50. This allows them to save $687.50 a month in their retirement accounts.

For five years they work on their fixer-upper house and each save 10% and their combined retirement savings grow to $97,378.81. When Carrie becomes pregnant and wants to be a stay-at-home mom, Dale has a salary of $36,000 and his employer provides hospital medical coverage.

They get life insurance and make a will. Dale reduces his 401(k) contribution to $100 per month, with his employer matching $50, for a total of $150 a month.

If they continue to save just a $150 a month in the 401(k) for the next thirty-two years they will have a cool million, about $1,123,039.43, even if Carrie doesn't return to work. Then, when Dale retires and they begin drawing on their account—assuming they take about 5%—they will receive an income of $4,679 a month. Social Security would give them another $1,000 to $2,000 of lifetime income.

The key is, start early. If they'd waited to start saving until after their child was born, they would have had to up their monthly saving to a whopping $700 at 7% to equal a $1,000,000 upon retirment.

What is wonderful about Dale and Carrie's story is that they funded tax deductible, tax deferred retirement plans so their savings and profit weren't taxed until they retired. Slow and steady thinking long-term wins the savings race.

Note: This all assumes they invest and earn 7%. Naturally they might each earn more or less then 7% depending on their investment returns. But it is certain, however, if they don't save, they will have nothing.

More on the "income" from our savings is discussed in future chapters.

This chapter is about **saving now.**

The same forces that are causing standards of living to rise and longevity to improve also promote loneliness. Steadily smaller households, made possible by prosperity, mean steadily less human interaction. Telecommuting, a personal convenience made possible by technology, means less human interaction. The culture of complaint, in which Americans and Europeans are encouraged to carp about ever smaller matters, drives us to take offense, which may cost friendships; the adulation of the family grievance, a prime topic of daytime television, drives us to find fault with those whom genetic chance made our relatives; the idealized images of romantic partners in entertainment and advertising can make a date, or a life, with an admirable but not extraordinary person seem a disappointment rather than a privilege.—GREGG EASTERBROOK, THE PROGRESS PARADOX

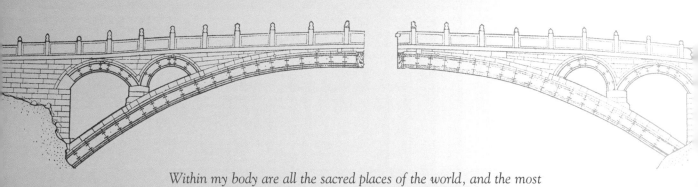

Within my body are all the sacred places of the world, and the most profound pilgrimage I can ever make is within my own body.
—SARAHA, NINTH CENTURY TANTRIC ADEPT

chapter 4

BUILDING A LEGACY BEGINS WITH OUR RELATIONSHIPS

Failure is an opportunity.
If you blame someone else, there is no end to the blame.
Therefore the Master fulfills her own obligations
and corrects her own mistakes.
She does what she needs to do and demands
nothing of others.—TAO TE CHING

Our legacy, the history of our future, is embedded in the relationships we have with our intimate community. We either nourish and respect those relationships, or we take them for granted. Our relationship choices color our future happiness much more than health or money do.

When I went through my divorce nine years ago, there was a brief period when I wondered if I would end up losing my home. Yet, in those trying times, in grasping for a sense of security, I counted more than one hundred couches at my disposal. That meant more than one hundred friends or family members I felt I could call upon for a night's rest, or more. Talk about feeling secure. Only my pride would have kept me from calling and asking for help, although many friends had already voiced their commitment to me.

We all live hectic lives which can prevent us from seeing the possibilities for connections in our daily life. We too often imagine that our friends are only an intimate few.

I disagree, and I disagree from experience.

I think we must look at each human encounter as if the person could become a dear lifetime friend. No matter if it's the grocery clerk, a wrong number on the telephone or the person at the end of the long line at the post office; be compassionate, be mindful. A Buddhist friend said, "If you brush against someone once, it is a person you have known a thousand lifetimes." Taking steps in the direction of a wonderful future means giving each person you meet the gift of respect, a smile and helpful action.

I want to be the recipient of honesty from my friends so that I can avoid consequences that might cause unintended harm. I hope my friends will feel free to ask me anything, free to tell me anything. Equally important, I want to be able to feel comfortable saying anything to them, including simply saying "No" in reply to their "Can you?" If I tell a friend I can't see them for lunch, or help them move, I shouldn't have to explain why. My friend should trust that I am unable to help, without a judgment on the validity of my decision.

Confucius said, "There are the three friends with whom there is gain and the three friends with whom there is loss. Befriend the honest, befriend the faithful, and befriend those who listen extensively and there is gain indeed. Befriend those who appear honorable, befriend those who are good at pleasing, and befriend those who appear to be artful in speech and there is loss indeed."

THE 100 COUCHES VISUALIZATION

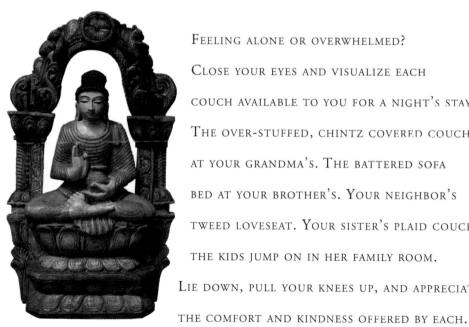

FEELING ALONE OR OVERWHELMED?

CLOSE YOUR EYES AND VISUALIZE EACH

COUCH AVAILABLE TO YOU FOR A NIGHT'S STAY.

THE OVER-STUFFED, CHINTZ COVERED COUCH

AT YOUR GRANDMA'S. THE BATTERED SOFA

BED AT YOUR BROTHER'S. YOUR NEIGHBOR'S

TWEED LOVESEAT. YOUR SISTER'S PLAID COUCH

THE KIDS JUMP ON IN HER FAMILY ROOM.

LIE DOWN, PULL YOUR KNEES UP, AND APPRECIATE

THE COMFORT AND KINDNESS OFFERED BY EACH.

Our Not So Perfect Partner

One intriguing theory about relationships is Imago Therapy, based on the work of Dr. Harville Hendrix. The basic principles of this therapy are that we were born whole and complete, but were inescapably wounded during childhood. We carry those wounds with us through life and subconsciously try to heal ourselves by selecting romantic partners who match up to form a composite image of our parents.

"When we fall in love, it's supposed to be forever," writes Hendrix. "We meet the person of our dreams and a magical transformation takes place within us. We feel alive, whole, connected to the world and the people in it. Then before we know it, that magical connection disappears! Where did it go?".

Imago Relationship Theory teaches that romantic love, which you experience at the beginning of a relationship, is the way our unconscious seeks to restore the feeling of joyful aliveness we felt as a young child. We are attracted to people who emotionally resemble our primary caretakers because we subconsciously believe they can satisfy our emotional needs. We call this 'finding our Imago match.'

Imago Therapy focuses on a person's natural desire for self-completion, especially as it relates to these unsettled childhood issues. In adulthood, when we are naively desperate for an opportunity to work out our childhood baggage, or so the theory goes, we are often attracted to partners who confront us with the same dilemmas we faced as children.

"However when we choose a partner who is our 'Imago match,' they resemble both the positive and the negative qualities of our primary caretakers. It's these negative qualities that create confusion and disillusionment when we realize that they are not able to meet our deepest emotional needs," according to Hendrix.

This can be a positive and healthy experience if we are successful in working out our childhood issues. Imago (literally, an 'image' of the person who can complete you) Therapy helps participants recognize defensive patterns, potential addictions and define an image of who their life-partner should be.

Hendrix writes, "Imago Relationship Therapy will help you become aware of the hidden agenda of romantic love, and to see that the conflict in your relationship is a wonderful opportunity for growth. The Imago dialogue provides a safe and supportive set of tools to explore these deep issues with your partner. The emotional bond initially created by romantic love is able to evolve into the powerful, lifelong bond that is real love."

I think most of the spiritual life is really a matter of relaxing—
letting go, ceasing to cling, ceasing to insist on our own way,
ceasing to tense ourselves up for this or against that.
—BEATRICE BRUTEAU, RADICAL OPTIMISM:
PRACTICAL SPIRITUALITY IN AN UNCERTAIN WORLD

See more about Imago Therapy at
www.gettingtheloveyouwant.com

Unrequited Generosity

Loving people often mysteriously find themselves emotionally paired with self-absorbed, irresponsible people. This is an environment ripe for one of society's most dreaded roles, the enabler.

Enabling and codependency are inextricably linked and it is easy for a giving person to fall under the spell of a taker, sapped of their natural creativity and life force through misplaced generosity. Are you an enabler? Are you happier caring for others than caring for yourself? When you do care for yourself, do you feel guilty about it?

Compassion and caring are certainly not character flaws, but neither is it healthy to **always** be the caregiver and **never** the recipient of care.

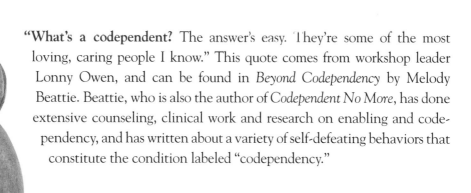

Teacher, author, poet, peace activist and Zen Buddhist monk Thich Nhat Hanh says, "When I was a novice, I could not understand why, if the world is filled with suffering, the Buddha has such a beautiful smile. Why isn't he disturbed by all the suffering? Later I discovered that the Buddha has enough understanding, calm, and strength; that is why the suffering does not overwhelm him. He is able to smile to suffering because he knows how to take care of it and to help transform it. We need to be aware of the suffering, but retain our clarity, calmness, and strength so we can help transform the situation. The ocean of tears cannot drown us if *karuna* (compassion) is there. That is why the Buddha's smile is possible."

"What's a codependent? The answer's easy. They're some of the most loving, caring people I know." This quote comes from workshop leader Lonny Owen, and can be found in *Beyond Codependency* by Melody Beattie. Beattie, who is also the author of *Codependent No More*, has done extensive counseling, clinical work and research on enabling and codependency, and has written about a variety of self-defeating behaviors that constitute the condition labeled "codependency."

But why do apparently rational people feel compelled to rescue others?

"**Many reasons,**" writes Beattie. "Most of us aren't even aware of what we're doing. Most of us truly believe we're helping. Some of us believe we have to rescue. We have confused ideas about what constitutes help and what doesn't... Many of us do not understand what we are responsible for and what we are not responsible for. We may believe we have to get into a tizzy when someone has a problem because it is our responsibility to do that... However, at the heart of most rescues is a demon: low self-worth. We rescue because we don't feel good about ourselves. Although the feelings are transient and artificial, caretaking provides us with a temporary hit of good feelings, self-worth and power."

The trouble with life is that it isn't cozy enough. In the baby part of ourselves, which every one of us still has, we all need to be hugged and cuddled... To be touched and held, to have our skin—that miraculous fine thin silken wrapper of our being—caressed, addressed, remembered, and cherished, is one of the greatest human requirements.
—DAPHNE ROSE KINGMA,
101 WAYS TO HAVE TRUE LOVE IN YOUR LIFE

Since we cannot change people, we must admit to being 100% responsible for accepting them as they are.

Should I change myself or accept myself as I am? Although self-change and self-acceptance appear to be in opposition, they're two essential sides of the same coin of self-transformation. When people come to my office for therapy they usually want to change themselves—or reshape their partner. Being unhappy with how things are, they're eager—if not desperate—to implement changes. But little do they realize that the key to creative change doesn't lie in our usual efforts to fix ourselves, poke at ourselves, or push ourselves. Just the opposite. The key to real and lasting change lies in the paradoxical art of accepting ourselves as we currently are.

—JOHN AMODEO, THE AUTHENTIC HEART:
AN EIGHTFOLD PATH TO MIDLIFE LOVE

It is not our responsibility to make people happy. We can be kind, funny, helpful, loving and smile sincerely. We can positively influence others to enjoy life, but only an individual can end the causes of his or her own suffering. When we try to step in and solve other people's problems, it's not only futile—it also robs them of the power and accomplishment they'd feel from solving their problems on their own.

It is up to you to decide who to allow into your life. **We are the gatekeepers of our soul** and have the right to choose those with whom we wish to share our intimate space.

The Noble Eightfold Path

right understanding

right intention

right speech

right action

right livelihood

right effort

right concentration

right mindfulness

Perhaps there should be a Ninth Noble Truth. **Right Association!**

chapter 5

TEN REASONS TO SAVE, PLUS ONE EXTRA

*Money, which represents the prose of life,
and which is hardly spoken of in parlors without an apology,
is, in its effects and laws, as beautiful as roses.* —RALPH WALDO EMERSON

Ideally, balanced and healthy spending habits are acquired at an early age so that you can avoid a cumbersome debt load and the resulting sentence to debtor's prison (a state of mind that makes it hard to smile and breathe comfortably). While old habits are hard to break, the following **Rules** will help to keep you from mismanaging your income, your assets and your debt. By following them, you can be assured of a more balanced life. On the other hand, reflection on the accompanying **Verses** will assure you of nothing—but with Taoism, that's kind of the point!

Rule One: Pay Yourself First

Save a minimum of 10% of your income in your IRA, 401(k) or another tax-favored retirement plan. This money, while often not convenient to withdraw, is nonetheless usually available if you have financial trouble. Savings is a habit. The average American makes about $2,500 monthly. If they saved $250 each month for thirty years and made 6% interest, they would have more than $250,000. If they earned a return of 10%, they would accrue more than $550,000 on that $90,000 investment.

Of course, investment returns cannot be guaranteed and the future is unknown, but I am certain that **if you save nothing you'll have nothing**. The most important financial habit is to save and invest 10% of your income. It should be invested wisely so that, as the Richest Man in Babylon stressed, "Gold can have children, and those children, children, and those children, children..."

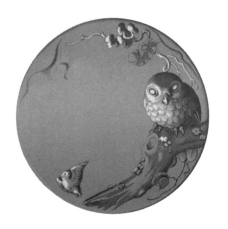

Verse One "The nameless is the beginning of heaven and earth. The name is the mother of the ten thousand things. Send your desires away and you will see the mystery. Be filled with desire and you will see only the manifestation."

Rule Two: Divine Surplus

Work to increase your monthly "divine surplus" and set aside 10% of your fixed budget for the "unexpected"—car repairs, a new boiler, a trip to see your ailing mother. Planner Jennifer Lazarus calls it "a bucket of money" for "this year only" type of expenses.

By putting it in your spending plan at the beginning of the year, you're admitting the reality that **stuff happens**.

The easiest way to do this is to directly deposit 10% of your paycheck into a money market fund at a discount broker, a bank or credit union savings account. Then, if you need it, simply transfer the money to your checking account. Depending on your job security, a revolving surplus of between 10% and 40% of your net yearly income is ideal. Self-employed individuals would be wise to keep a surplus of upwards of 25%, due to the sometimes unstable nature of their work. Those contractually employed by the government or large corporations can usually get away with a 10% surplus.

> *Verse Two "Deny nothing to the ten thousand things. Nourish them without claiming authority, benefit them without demanding gratitude, do the work, then move on. And, the fruits of your labor will last forever."*

Rule Three: Karma

In the spirit of generosity discussed throughout this book, set aside 10% of your budget for family, friends, charities, tithing, gifts and helping others. It's the right thing to do, and karma will reward you. Security comes from good, committed relationships, relationships that are built on our sincere acts of kindness, generosity and compassion. So pay yourself first, then, with gratitude, save 10% for others.

Verse Three "Not exalting the talented prevents rivalry.
Not valuing goods that are hard to obtain prevents stealing.
Not displaying desirable things prevents confusion of the heart."

Rule Four: The Egg

As you invest, be sure to park some of your assets in a liquid, interest-bearing account, such as a money market higher yield savings. Ideally, your liquid savings should equal six months of your budget. **Do that and, most likely, you'll never go into unanticipated debt.**

This means that if your total monthly expenses (including mortgage, school loans, charity, savings, food, entertainment, utilities—everything) total $4,000, you will need to accumulate $24,000 as a security valve. If you earn $5,000 monthly ($1,000 surplus each month) and want a new car that costs $400 a month, you should save the down payment so you don't dip into your six-month reserve fund. Feel free to consider CDs and conservative mutual funds as part of your liquid assets when faced with setting up your reserve fund. If you have some stock-only portfolios, they should only be counted on for half their current value.

> *Verse Four "The Tao is like an empty bowl, yet it may be used without ever needing to be filled. It is the deep and unfathomable source of the ten thousand things. Blunt the sharpness. Untie the knot. Soften the glare. Settle with the dust."*

Rule Five: Balance

Debt is not a portender of the road to ruin, but life lasts a long time. Absolutely debt-free is the other extreme from ruin. Think balance. Consolidate your home, investment properties, home improvements and other long-term assets into one big loan with a fixed interest rate and the minimum required payment. (A thirty-year mortage, for example.)

> From Verse Five *"The space between heaven and earth is like a bellows. It is empty and yet never exhausted. The more it works the more comes out. Many words lead to exhaustion. Better to hold fast to your center."*

Rule Six: The Kindness of Strangers

Take full advantage of the fact that the interest on home loans is tax-deductible. Restructure your credit card bills to take advantage of the equity in your home, but vow to not let your consumer debt pile up again.

> Verse Six *"The valley spirit never dies. It is the unknown first mother, whose gate is the root from which grew heaven and earth. It is dimly seen, yet always present. Draw from it all you wish; it will never run dry."*

Rule Seven: Common Sense

Never pay down your home interest rate by paying points. Instead, go for a fixed rate on a fifteen- to thirty-year mortgage that has no points. The idea is to always allow yourself to refinance when interest rates fall.

Verse Seven "Heaven and earth last forever. The reason why heaven and earth last forever is that they do not live for themselves. Hence, they last forever."

Rule Eight: Own Yourself

Aspire to be your own banker by paying cash for cars, home repairs, remodeling, boats, etc., to avoid high interest costs. When anticipating a large purchase, begin saving in a liquid savings or money market account so that when the time comes, ample cash is available.

Verse Eight "The highest good is like water. For water benefits the ten thousand things without striving. It settles in places that people avoid and so is like the Tao."

Rule Nine: Karma Kards

Maintain control over your "instant karma" cards (credit cards). Again, like other debt vehicles, credit cards offer wonderful freedom and quite often there are frequent flyer miles to accrue, charities to benefit and other perks. But be careful. Adhere to the following dharma for help in balanced credit card use: If you can't pay off the balance each month, cut them up and cancel them.

> *Verse Nine "Better to stop in time than to fill to the brim.*
> *Hone a blade to the sharpest point and it will soon be blunt.*
> *Fill your house with gold and jade, and no one can protect it.*
> *Be prideful about wealth and position, and you bring disasters upon*
> *yourself. Retire when the work is done. This is the way of heaven."*

Rule Ten: Honor Your Commitments

Keep your promises, even at difficult moments when the pressure to consume is strongest. Don't play the irresponsible game of rationalizing your aberrant spending behavior. Integrity is keeping a promise even after you've had a change of heart. If you sign the loan application, accept the credit card or close the deal with the car dealer, it's your karma to live up to the commitment. Occasionally, legitimate problems arise and it is necessary to appeal to your banker for relief. Bankers are prepared for calls like this, so don't wait too long.

> *Verse Ten "While carrying your active life on your head*
> *can you embrace the quiet spirit in your arms, and not let go?"*

And One More: Action

Don't wait until you lose your job or have a medical crisis to get your life in order. Do it now! Banks will loan you money when you "don't need it" so to speak, but too often decline when difficulties arise. This is reality.

Verse Eleven "Clay is shaped into a vessel; yet, it is the emptiness within that makes it useful. Doors and windows are cut for a room; yet it is the space where there is nothing that makes it useful. Therefore, though advantage comes from what is; usefulness comes from what is not."

Knowing these rules doesn't do any good unless you implement them—**Do It Now!**

Nothing happens until something moves.
—ALBERT EINSTEIN

A big fire was destroying the forest. All the animals fled, except the
hummingbird. It flew to the river, picked up one drop of water in its
tiny beak, flew back, and poured that drop on the fire. Again and
again it returned to the river, each time scooping up a single drop and
pouring it on the fire. The other animals watched from the far shore,
laughing and mocking. The harder they laughed, the harder
the hummingbird worked. 'Just what do you think you're doing?'
the animals asked. Without stopping her work, she answered calmly,
'I'm doing what I can.' That's all any of us can do: what we can.

—WANGARI MAATHAI, 2004 WINNER OF THE NOBEL PEACE PRIZE

chapter 6

401(K)S
HOW THEY WORK,
HOW TO WORK THEM

At first, people refuse to believe that a strange new thing can be done,
and then they begin to hope it can be done. Then they see it can be done—
then it is done and all the world wonders why it was not done centuries ago.
—FRANCES HODGSON BURNETT

Our good intentions are great, but have power only when we act on
them. A journey of a thousand miles begins with the mind saying,
"Foot move, foot move, quiet lazy thoughts, silence can't thoughts!"
We must move ahead and learn.

See pages 28-29

Remember that story about Dale and Carrie who were able to retire at sixty-five with over a million dollars in the bank? They did that through saving in Dale's 401(k) plan, using the power of time and compound interest. Many self-made millionaires get their start this way: it's the fastest and easiest way to save for retirement. Dale's employer, like most, offered a 401(k) plan, and Carrie's employer, a school, offered a 403(b) plan (which is also used by non-profit organizations) as part of their benefits package.

Money is like a sixth sense without which you cannot make a complete use of the other five.—W. SOMERSET MAUGHAM

How does it work?

You put a percentage of your pre-tax paycheck into the plan each month, and your employer may match a portion of your contributions, up to a certain limit.

Since the money going into the plan isn't taxed, you have reduced your income, saving on taxes.

Then your boss adds a matching amount of money to your savings, on top of your pay. For example, if you are contributing $100 each month, and your company matches 50%, then they will put an additional $50, free of tax (and completely separate from your paycheck), into your account.

You now have $150 in your retirement account—earning an instant 50% increase on your investment!

To compare the difference between a 401(k) type plan and a savings investment plan, here are the numbers.

Let's say you make $50,000 a year and are in the 25% tax bracket.

Using the 401(k) plan, and contributing the $100 monthly from the above example, you are lowering your annual taxable income by $1200, saving $300 in taxes for the year.

Investing the $150 matched contribution for twenty years, at say 8%, yields you $88,000 by retirement.

Assuming income tax at retirement of 25%, you would have $66,000 left to spend.

Even better– by also investing that annual tax savings of $300, you can have an extra $14,000 to add to your returns—a tidy little sum indeed.

If, on the other hand, you don't use the 401(k) plan, that original $100 becomes $75 after taxes, giving you only a $44,000 return in twenty years, a sum which might be subject to some taxes at retirement.

Although 401(k) and similar plans are a great place to start your retirement investments, one major drawback is that many do not offer real, total return, make-money-don't-lose-it strategies for their investors to choose from.

Often employers are passive and choose the well-known, follow-the-crowd mutual fund that includes the investment company's products. These plans are based upon asset-type investment systems rather than a skills-based system.

Asset-based systems are usually full of indexed funds or funds benchmarked to an index.

An index fund is a group of stocks which are the same as those in an index, such as the S&P 500 index, rather than a fund made up of hand chosen stocks created by a fund manager.

If your employer's investment options look like this, you'll have to be your own manager until they decide to "get real" and allow some total return oriented funds.

See a current list of indexed funds at www.zenvesting.com

Four Do-It-Yourself Actions to Ensure Success For Your 401(k)

1. Commit to staying your course of investing for at least five years. Hopefully, your employers will add some skill-based managers to your roundup and then you can switch to those managers. Even if your plan deposits are 100% invested in guaranteed accounts or at money market rates because of tax savings, you're usually way ahead of any other option for wealth accumulation.

2. Fund the plan to the maximum allowed by your company and the government.

   Here is a handy calculator: www.calcxml.com/do/qua09

3. If you are allowed unlimited rebalancing options and are making consistent deposits, try to rebalance at least quarterly. Otherwise, do so on yield changes.

4. Use managed funds.

   See www.zenvesting.com for guides to managed funds.

The Paradox of Our Age

We have bigger houses
and smaller families;
more convenience, but less time.

We have degrees, but less sense;
more knowledge, but less judgment;
more experts, but more problems;
more medicine, but less healthiness.

We have been all the way to the moon
and back, but have trouble crossing the street
to meet the new neighbor.

We built more computers to hold more
information to produce more copies than ever,
but have less communication.

We have become long on quantity,
but short on quality.

These are times of fast foods,
and slow digestion;
tall men and short characters;
steep profits and shallow relationships.

It is time when there is much in the window
and nothing in the room.

—HIS HOLINESS THE XIVTH DALAI LAMA

chapter 7

NO BETTER PLACE THAN HOME

Happiness, not in another place, but this place…
not for another hour, but this hour.—WALT WHITMAN

Home is where the kitchen table is. It can be a trailer, a condo or a clapboard house. It can be in a village, a neighborhood, a subdivision or out in the country. Regardless of what or where it is, your home is the place where you sleep and eat. It's where you feel safe, relaxed and comfortable. **A home is not an investment** despite what realtors, mortgage brokers, real estate books, articles and financial consultants will tell you. Investments are to store value, grow and provide income; they are purchased purely for that purpose. The purpose of your home is to provide you with shelter. **You buy a home to live in it.**

"I would like you to visit my family's home," said Kuldee, our tut tut (rickshaw) driver. My wife Amy responded, "Sure, we would love to," to the man who had courageously whisked us through Delhi noisy streets. We found Kuldee's happy optimism and intense desire to give his children a better life through education inspiring—he worked twelve-hour days, six and a half days a week, so that his children could attend private school.

As we sat drinking tea with Kuldee and his gracious wife, his newborn baby, his mother, his brother and his brother's wife, I felt pride, happiness, love and contentment radiating from the windowless ten by twenty foot room they called home.

The door was open to the crowded alley, and like all of Delhi it was a noisy and dusty place. As Amy chatted with Kuldee's wife and mother-in-law, I thought about the homes and houses I had seen in my life: our lovely home in Michigan, a ten thousand square foot house I'd been to recently. There were the homes I'd visited in Guatemala's slums and neighborhoods, and Amy's description of dwellings from her recent trip to rural Nigeria to immunize kids against polio. **All of this made me realize that what constitutes a home is really about what you think you deserve.** People can live in a trailers, tents, condos, villas, ranches—and be happy. So please rethink your home paradigm. Come to terms with your home as it is regarding size, shape, and location and try to relax about any "shoulds" or "gotta haves."

Sociologists have long assumed that rising income does not necessarily confer rising happiness owing to 'reference anxiety,' a fancy term for keeping up with the Joneses. As incomes rise, people stop thinking, 'Does my house meet my needs?' and instead, 'Is my house nicer than the neighbor's?' Here, research suggest, the essential element is an expectation of more. A person with a middling but rising income may be happier than a person with high but stagnant income. A person with a small house who expects to move into a medium-sized house may be happier than a person with a large house who knows it is the largest he will ever own.

—Gregg Easterbrook, *The Progress Paradox*

In Mali West Africa the Natomos family of eleven shares two mud houses that would provide a moderate "efficiency" apartment for an adult couple in urban USA. Their total possessions, aside from the clothes they wear in their family portrait in Material World, number forty including a 'Ritual Cane.'

Bill Gates, billed as the world's richest private individual, a few years ago moved into his 40,000 square-foot "ecology house" sliding down a west-facing hill to the edge of a Seattle lake. His family of four (not counting nanny and multiple unidentified support staff) consume more than ten thousand square feet per person. At the standards of the Natomos, an extended family of about 450 people could live in Bill's house. . .

Social sermons about inequality are not the point of this comparison. What it raises are questions of what constitutes a house and how does it contribute to the well-being of those who live in it... The Gates and Natomos share much once they cross the boundary to their property...the worst of weather is excluded from the family space. At mealtimes the family can gather to share food and talk with only those they choose to invite. At night each person has a sheltered place to rest. When they leave during the day their possessions remain behind awaiting the owner's return. For the children, home is the place where they are fed, loved, guided and eventually released to form their own family. For the adults it's where love, sharing of the goods and infor-mation gained in the outside community, support and binds the family.

Home then, molds creation of personal and family history and plans as well as per-mits the activities that define family life. While it is never perfect, it provides a personal Utopia in each member's organization of memory and vision of the future. For the Natomos and Gates, the function is the same. What happens within the family's walls, however malleable, will still be the foundation of each new member's vision and their creation of a personal utopia. It will undoubtedly expand and morph, but it will always start at home."

—James Mitchell, "Personal Utopia, Technology's Effect on the Meaning of Home" from *Viable Utopian Ideas: Shaping a Better World*

While homes do have investment characteristics, don't make the mistake of believing that your home is your investment portfolio. Buying a home as an "investment" flies in the face of good sense and ultimately gets you off track. There's every possibility that your "good investment" will make you miserable because each decorating and remodeling decision will be dependent on resale value as opposed to what you really want.

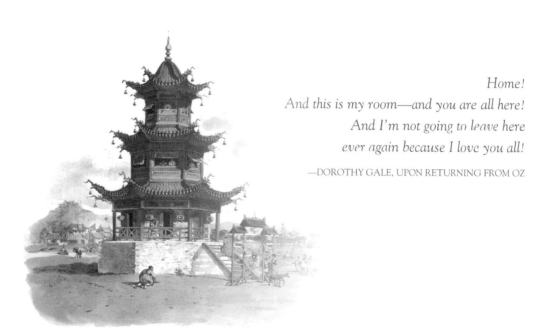

Home!
And this is my room—and you are all here!
And I'm not going to leave here
ever again because I love you all!

—DOROTHY GALE, UPON RETURNING FROM OZ

After 25 years of helping people design, build and remodel their homes, I've become convinced that understanding the 'emotional architecture' a client brings to a project is a critical part of designing a house that feels like a home. One day I experienced an epiphany. I was (away from home) converting a group of historic buildings into a country inn. Alone all week, I had plenty of time to think. In the evenings I would sit in an old rocking chair on the wood plank porch. I found myself inexplicably happy. Everything seemed right with the world as I rocked on that porch. I began to ask myself why, and before long I uncovered the source of my unexplained peace of mind.

I remembered a place from my childhood...my great grandfather's porch. When I was a young child, I spent a lot of time on that porch. I cannot remember a time in my life when I felt more loved or appreciated. Suddenly I understood why I kept returning to historic restoration work even though, truth be told, it was less profitable than my other building ventures. I realized then that we all view the world through a broad set of internal associations most, but not all, from our childhood. This internal landscape determines how we respond emotionally to the architecture in our surroundings.

Now, eight years later, I live in another old farmhouse. I'm happy and feel very much at home. Built in the 1840's, the restoration is still not complete. The downstairs is cold in the winter and the upstairs is a hothouse in the summer. Bugs find it easy to get in and the AC finds it easy to get out. The old place requires constant maintenance. You would think these things would be annoying, but I sit on my porch in the evenings and think about how lucky I am.

—Chris Travis, managing partner of Round Top Architects

Purchasing a home, for most people, represents the largest budgetary item, the biggest financial commitment, and therefore one of the most important decisions they'll ever make.

Your job is to make sure there is no better place than home.

Buy or Rent?

Get over it—you don't have to own the building you're living in for it to be a true home. Deciding to buy or rent a home depends on how long you plan to be there.

Most people like the stability of ownership, but the decision to purchase or not shouldn't hinge on finances alone, rather the considerations of comfort and lifestyle. A home is one of the cornerstones of a balanced life and unlike most purchases, its purchase should be an attitudinal or emotional decision.

Naturally, if you don't like the idea of being tied down, renting is probably the best bet. And, it usually makes sense to purchase your home if you plan to stay at least four years or more.

Nowhere in my experience do values intersect with money more than the home purchase decision. Realize that we trade time for money and each of us must balance how much we will work to afford the home we want. It's perfectly okay to forego college savings, retirement contributions, or even the purchase of more home if we admit the potential consequences of paying up.

There are many methods of figuring the economic sense of buying versus renting. See www.zenvesting.com for more information and some calculators.

Buying more home could mean having to work longer into "retirement," borrowing to help your children with college, or asking them to pay for their own way.

Also, and this is a big one, don't assume your house is going to be worth that much more in the future just because you paid up. The housing market is as fickle as fashion: one day big houses on big lots are in; the next day downtown condos or townhouses are all the fad.

Selling Your Home

In the US, the sale of a primary home is generally not reported on your tax returns unless the gain exceeds an "exclusion amount." What does that mean? Currently, the IRS has provided for taxpayers the ability to exclude from their reported income up to $250,000 of the profit off the sale of the home for single taxpayers, or $500,000 for those who are married and filing jointly, but only if the following ownership and use requirements are met:

> **Both spouses must have owned and used the home as their principal residence for at least two out of the five years prior to the sale.**
> **In addition, each spouse is limited in frequency to selling a home no more than once every two years.**

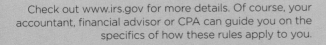

Check out www.irs.gov for more details. Of course, your accountant, financial advisor or CPA can guide you on the specifics of how these rules apply to you.

A single individual must also meet the same requirements for ownership, use and frequency of sale.

Even though the exclusion rules have removed a lot of the complexity from the calculation and reporting requirements on the sale of your home, it is still very important to track any improvements on it. Home improvements can aid you in staying under the gain/exclusion limits.

Throw every home improvements receipt in a "home improvements" file.

When you go to sell your home add them up and find your cost basis.

A common question asked of accountants and tax preparers is how exclusion rules apply to the sale of your second home. Unfortunately, the gain/exclusion applies only to your primary residence. The IRS has issued final regulations that say when a taxpayer alternates between two residences, the one that is used for a majority of the time during the year will ordinarily be considered the principal residence.

If there is any question of which home is your primary residence, the IRS will use relevant factors such as place of employment, where your children go to school, the address listed on your federal and state tax returns, driver's license, automobile registration and voter registration card, mailing address for bills and correspondence, the location of banks and religious organizations and recreational clubs with which you are affiliated.

According to R'Yonah, the verse contrasts two types of debtors. One who does not repay a loan is not deemed evil if he is really destitute and unable to pay. The evil exists if he borrowed without having objectively evaluated his ability to make restitution. The righteous person, on the other hand, assumes only as much of an obligation as he feels he can reasonably handle. While one who pays his debts is only fulfilling an obligation for which he deserves no gratitude or honor, an honorable borrower returns the money graciously and earns the gratitude and love of his creditors. Hence, he is referred to as a righteous person.

—MOSHE LIEBER, *THE PIRKEI AVOS TREASURY: ETHICS OF THE FATHERS*

KARMA & DEBT

*Reality is far more vicious than Russian roulette. First, it delivers the fatal
bullet rather infrequently, like a revolver that would have hundreds,
even thousands of chambers instead of six. After a few dozen tries,
one forgets about the existence of a bullet, under a numbing sense of security.*
—NASSIM NICHOLAS TALEB, FOOLED BY RANDOMNESS

Your debts are spiraling out of control. You unwisely listened to the salesman who said, "This is an investment" when he pitched you jewelry, a fancier car or a house that's more than you can afford. Now you're living off credit cards to make ends meet. Although you can blame society, your parents, or your spouse for your problems, the truth is that you are experiencing karma. This notion may require a radical shift in viewpoint, but you must recognize that you, and only you, are responsible for the actions that created your current financial situation. **You can't move forward until you rid yourself of blaming society or others for your debt.**

Here are three straightforward steps toward this goal:

Realize that your debt is your problem, caused by your actions. Blame no one!

Forgive yourself and move forward. Own up to the idea that you are responsible.

Take your debt very seriously. Make it a real part of your life.

If you've read this far, you may have realized that your debt stops you from building any kind of wealth. The goal is to manage your debt consistently while taking into consideration the reality of your life.

How do you know if your debts are excessive?
Simple! Ask yourself two questions:

Would I sleep better and be more relaxed if I only had my mortgage to worry about?

Would I sleep better and be more relaxed if I was debt free?

The first practical step that an individual can take to free himself from the thrall of money is not to turn away from it, but to take it even more seriously, to study himself in the very midst of the world of money, but to study himself with such diligence and concern that the very act of self-study becomes as vivid and intense as the desires and fears he is studying.

—JACOB NEEDLEMAN

Good Debt, Bad Debt

Let's say that hard times or past mistakes have driven you into debt. Some debt is worse than others. "Good" debt is money you have borrowed for secure, long-term gains such as student loans, which provide an education and the potential for more income, or a reasonable bank mortgage, which gives you and your family a home. Your focus should be on getting rid of "bad" debt: money borrowed on credit cards or retail store cards, or high monthly payments for unnecessarily expensive items that quickly lose their value.

Good Debt

- A house you can afford.
- Education & enhancing your skills.
- Large Items, as long as total payments for debt is under 25% of your family's budget if you earn less than $6,000 monthly, 30% if you earn more.

Best To Save Up To Buy

- Luxury items such as boats, cameras, jewelry, snowmobiles.
- Entertainment items such as TVs, music, video games.
- Vacations.
- Children's education—or make it a part of your budget.
- Cars.

Your first step is to make an inventory of what you owe, the minimum payment, the interest rate, and your payment schedule. Once you do that, focus on getting out of the high-interest rate cards first. (As a cautionary note, be sure to watch the interest rates on your credit cards—they can change without notice, but a call to the credit card company can sometimes help.)

	Amount Owing	Current Interest Rate	Monthly Payment Amount	Payment Due Date	Amount and Date Paid
Notes					
Credit Card One					
Credit Card Two					
Credit Card Three					
First Home Mortgage					
Second Mortgage					
Student Loan One					
Student Loan Two					
First Car Payment					
Second Car Payment					
Other					
Other					

Now, because interest rates are highest on unsecured debt, you'll want to consolidate the money owed on credit cards with a low-interest home equity loan on your house, if you have one. To avoid building up a credit card balance again—and potentially lose your home because of missed payments on the equity loan—make sure to close all your credit card accounts. Use a debit card for all purchases, or, if you absolutely feel you need a credit card, call the company and have them lower your credit limit to an amount that you can pay off each month.

Sam and Karen

Here's a scenario of a couple that got in over their heads. Sam and Karen overstretched to buy their home—a common mistake—and now realize that after a year, they are drawing about $1,000 monthly on credit cards to make ends meet.

Sam and Karen argue a lot about money. They are thinking about seeing a bankruptcy lawyer, but don't like the "karma" in stiffing anyone, even the nameless, soulless credit card companies. What to do?

What they did—and what you'll need to do too—was to take a look at each expense and see where they could lower monthly payments enough to make ends meet, without borrowing on credit cards.

First, here's a snapshot of their finances:

- Sam is a telemarketer and makes $38,000 after taxes.

- Karen is a web designer. Her take-home pay is $28,000.

- They have no children, zero savings, and have cashed in their retirement accounts to survive.

- Their employee benefits include disability and medical insurance.

Second, here is a table of their monthly expenses:

Asset	Interest	Value	Loan	Monthly payment
Home (29 years left)	6%	$385,000	$359,000	$2,185
Auto #1 (45 months left)	4.8%	10,000	12,000	292
Auto #2 (18 months left)	4.8%	6,000	6,000	360
School loan (42 months left)	7%	n/a	58,000	1,561
Credit cards (interest only)	12%	n/a	17,000	170
Loan from parents	0%	n/a	90,000	Unable to pay on loan

Total of Monthly Payments: $4568

Finally, here are Sam and Karen's goals:

- Stop borrowing to make ends meet.

- Save for the future.

- Stop feeling so stressed.

- Get their budget to work after debts are reduced.

- Relax and enjoy life!

I don't want to get to the end of my life and find
that I lived just the length of it. I want to have lived
the width of it as well. —DIANE ACKERMAN

Paying off debt versus investing in your retirement

Many people argue that it's more important to pay off a high-interest credit card before you begin investing in retirement. That's because the interest you pay on a credit cards—twelve percent and up—might be higher than the interest you'll receive on any investment. This becomes less of an issue if you can consolidate the high-interest credit card balance into a home equity loan. Then, you can split your "savings" into paying off a credit card and investing in your retirement. If this isn't possible, you should aggressively pay off the credit card and then get busy saving.

After a lengthy discussion with a fee-only adviser, Sam and Karen decided to do the following:

Keep the home.
No net change

Cut gasoline costs. Sam commutes forty-eight miles each way to his job, which costs $125 a week in gas costs alone. Sam's employer agreed to allow Sam to try "telecommuting" for three months, with Sam coming into the office on Fridays. He has guaranteed Sam a desk if it doesn't work out.
Savings: $500 monthly

Cut the car payment. Sam and Karen decided they could live with one car. Sam will borrow Karen's car each Friday for his drive into work and Karen will carpool that day. Sam went back to the dealer and said, "Here's my car. You can have it and the loan payment book and I'd like to pay off what I owe." The dealer took the car and figured the "excess loan value"—or what Sam owed—minus the value of the car ($2,000). To pay it off, Sam will make twenty monthly payments of $100.
Savings: $252 (payment, maintenance and insurance)

Refinance Karen's car. Karen went to the auto dealership and refinanced her car to a lower payment by renegotiating the loan period to thirty-six months and raising her interest rate from 4.8% to 6% over thirty-six months. That reduced her payment from $360 to $185.
Savings: $175 monthly

Restructure the $58,000 college loan. Sam went to his college loan company (Karen went along for moral support) and said: "Here's the reality. I have $388 I can afford to spend on my school loan each month. Can you make it work for me?" The company consented to charge Sam interest payment only on the loan for five years and to renegotiate the loan after that. His new payment is $388.
Savings: $1,173 monthly

Make good on loan from parents: Sam got a call from Mom who said Dad is losing sleep over the $90,000 loan they made to them—his parents' entire nest egg for retirement. They met and Sam made a commitment to pay them $500 monthly for the rest of his parents' lives.

Add to budget: $500 monthly

Restructure credit card payments. Sam and Karen called their credit card companies and negotiated a 7% interest rate with $340 monthly payments. They will have the cards paid off in five years. They closed the accounts of all but one credit card they committed to using only for emergencies and travel.

Add to budget: $170 monthly

Start saving for retirement. Karen and Sam filled out The Gentle Budgeting Worksheet (page 183) and both started to put $50 monthly into their employee's 401(k) plan.

Add to budget: $100 monthly

Make long-term commitments to each other. Karen and Sam realized they were dependent on each other and each bought a $250,000 ten-year term insurance policy with low load insurance. They made Karen's parents a $100,000 beneficiary in each of their policies.

Add to budget: $38 monthly

Plan for the future. They made wills using a lawyer Karen had designed a site for (in trade) and celebrated by getting the sports and sci-fi packages and canceling HBO.

No net change

Total savings: $1292 monthly

The
past is not a
burden; it is a scaffold which brought
us to this day. We are free to be
who we are—to create our own life
out of our past and out of the present.
We are our ancestors. When we heal ourselves,
we also heal our ancestors, our grandmothers, our
grandfathers and our children.

—RITA PITKA BLUMENSTEIN,
A YUP'IK ELDER WHO HAS BECOME
THE FIRST CERTIFIED TRADITIONAL
DOCTOR IN ALASKA, AS QUOTED IN
WORLD PULSE
MAGAZINE

chapter 9

INSURING YOUR HAPPINESS

*God breaks the heart again and again
and again until it stays open.*
—HAZRAT INAYAT KHAN, FOUNDER OF THE SUFI ORDER
INTERNATIONAL, AS QUOTED IN *THE EXQUISITE RISK:
DARING TO LIVE AN AUTHENTIC LIFE* BY MARK NEPO

Twenty-eight years ago I received the phone call telling me that my father had lost his yearlong battle with adrenal cancer. We had been expecting Dad's death, but the news was still painful, and my thoughts went instantly to my mother who now had my four younger siblings at home to look after. Fortunately, what could have been a financial disaster was prevented because of Dad's foresight and planning.

Unlike some families, who are dealing with both the loss of a loved one and a major breadwinner, my family was able to concentrate on healing, loving and supporting Dad and each other through the illness and after. His disability insurance had paid the mortgage and other bills for the year he was fighting cancer, while his medical insurance covered all but a couple hundred dollars of his $60,000 medical expenses. An adequate nest egg freed Mom from a stressful work-schedule and allowed her more time with her young family. Also, she did not have to worry about probate or inflexible court-ordered asset protection rules because they had made simple wills and titled the house correctly. So, although Mom and Dad weren't financially "rich"—he never made more than $40,000 a year and she $20,000—they had planned well, and that was a blessing for our family in that stressful time.

Today, insurance planning is much less expensive and easier than ever. Many employers have disability insurance, group life insurance and group hospital medical to build a solid insurance plan from. In my father's case, the insurance policies and the simple yet solid estate-planning were truly the most considerate love letter he could have written. Dad's responsible actions showed his love and commitment to his family, even after he was gone.

It is wonderful to be a cloud, but it is also wonderful to be the rain. It is also wonderful to be the snow or water. If the cloud remembers this, then when the cloud is about to transform and continue in the form of rain, it will not be so frightened.—THICH NHAT HANH, NO DEATH, NO FEAR: COMFORTING WISDOM FOR LIFE

Defining Risk

Insurance is a powerful, effective tool when used judiciously. Basically, it is a means of reducing or limiting a risk by dividing the loss among many individuals. It can be used to your advantage when you keep in mind the following two points.

First, you should not insure against predictable risks in which the financial effect would be modest, such as the potential need for new eyeglasses or a capped tooth. These minor sums should be taken care of by the reserve fund suggested in Chapter 3, Achieving Independence. Only transfer risks that would harm your financial well-being. It's fiscally wise to purchase insurance for the $10,000, $100,000 or $1,000,000 calamities, not the small, incidental expenses.

Second, choosing large deductibles will greatly reduce the cost of insurance while still fulfilling its purpose. Because commissions, accounting, administration, marketing and overhead expenses are all paid out of premiums, insurers can only give back a certain percentage of your premium (the price you pay for the insurance). A sad fact of the insurance industry is the conflict of interest caused by commissions paid to agents. Keep this in mind when an agent recommends a policy with a modest or zero deductible but higher premiums, as they may be doing so because of the bigger commission they will receive.

For example, you can greatly reduce your premiums when purchasing car insurance by accepting a $500 or $1,000 deductible. So if you can handle the $500 cost of replacing your car window, then choose a $500 deductible on the insurance, and take advantage of the savings in monthly premiums.

Property and Liability Insurance

Complicated, ever-changing policies require locating an honest, expert insurance agent. If possible, choose one who is well respected, experienced, organized, ethical and, if you can find one, fee-only. Let them know that you are interested in purchasing policies that cover you against risks that are substantial, no matter how remote that risk. It is important to find out which risks the policy does not cover, and which are being transferred to you or are not covered. You can, at that point, decide whether the risks you will be assuming are manageable. If not, transfer them to an insurance company. Periodically, get a second opinion on your coverage and have it "bid" out. Agents often get complacent about lowering your costs and figure you must be happy if you have not asked for a better, lower-cost insurance solution.

Umbrella Liability Coverage

Once you have some assets to protect, you should buy personal umbrella liability insurance (usually a $1 million to $3 million benefit) to provide catastrophic coverage over and above the required underlying limit on home and auto policies. Like an umbrella, it shields you from the cracks and loopholes in your regular auto and home insurance policies, especially in the case of lawsuits.

If you rent and own assets of value, such as a camera, furniture, entertainment equipment, a computer and so forth, you should get renter's insurance. It's easy to get and reasonable—just call a good agent.

Here are additional tips from the Health Insurance Resource Center: www.healthinsurance.org

Health Insurance

It's important to start with a comprehensive, major medical policy that covers reasonable hospital and medical expenses and includes a deductible and stop loss provision. Remember, each policy varies, so ask your agent for details.

Typically, with a health insurance policy, there are deductibles for each family member, plus an overall deductible for the family. For example, you might have four family members, each with a deductible of $500, and a capped $1,000 deductible for the entire family. So, once two members of the family hit the $500 deductible, the insurance company begins to reimburse all the family members for covered services.

After you meet the deductible, you usually have what's called co-insurance. The insurance company will pay 80% of the bill and you pay 20%. A stop loss insurance provision says that you'll pay no more than a certain amount—say $1,000—after the co-insurance kicks in.

Here's an example of how the stop loss provision works.

Let's say you've met your deductible of $500 and you get a medical bill for $10,000. The insurance company will cover $8,000 and without a stop loss provision, you would pay $2,000. With a stop loss provision of $1,000, you'd only have to pay $1,000 and the insurance company would pick up the remainder.

Your policy should pay private or semi-private room charges and the full cost of unlimited stays in intensive care, burn and cardiac care units. Also, absolutely make sure your policy covers pre-existing conditions and has a maximum limit of no less than $500,000 (a million is more reasonable). Cancellation protection should be included in the policy's contract.

Come to peace with risk and change. Goethe, the German philosopher, reminds us, "that the moment one definitely commits oneself, then Providence moves, too. All sorts of things occur to help one that would never otherwise have occurred…all manner of unforeseen incidents and meetings and material assistance, which no man could have dreamed would have come his way. Whatever you can do, or dream, you can begin it. Boldness has genius, power and magic in it. Begin it now."
—MARGARET A. LULIC, *WHO WE COULD BE AT WORK*

As with all insurance policies it is always wise to ask your insurance advisor for a list of the policy limitations and charges your policy will not cover. Standard policy exclusions would be war, self-inflicted injuries, medical expenses that had no costs and expenses covered by a Veterans Affairs hospital, etc.

Insurance For Life on page 184 is a worksheet that can help you determine whether or not you need life insurance

Life Insurance

Not everyone needs life insurance, although life insurance agents might like to think so. If you are single with no dependents, it's one expense you don't have to worry about. If you have children or a spouse who depend on you and would suffer financially if you died, you need it. However, if you have amassed a large fortune, your death would not cause economic havoc in anyone's life because you have already built up a sizable net worth that could produce income.

Also, many people go wrong by looking only at a specific amount of death benefit, rather than what the death benefit will provide in monthly income. Income is the key. In England they don't call a (financially) rich person a millionaire; they call them a "hundred thousand pounder," meaning that she's got £100,000 of annual income. It is not the amount of assets, but the purchasing power those assets can generate.

Oh, that my monk's robes
were wide enough
to gather up
all the people in this
floating world.
—RYOKAN

Let's say, for example, that a spouse, who is insured for $1 million, tragically dies before the couple's three children attend college. Assuming a 6% return on $1 million, the family will receive $60,000 each year from the interest on the principal. The surviving spouse can add their working salary to that, in addition to Social Security benefits.

Over time, inflation will influence the value of any income stream that is not structured to offset a rising cost of living. Because of this fact of life, your assets should earn more than 6%, potentially allowing income to increase every year to help offset inflation. In today's environment of low interest rates, low dividend yields on stocks and low income yields on real estate, a 6% return could be considered aggressive—and it is. History shows, however, that markets are cyclical, so a higher yield on investments can be expected in the future.

Make it a habit to check your insurance coverage often. Since it is unnecessary to pay for a benefit you don't need, you should decrease the amount of insurance you own as your net worth increases. **The goal is to eventually not need much insurance because your net worth is so high.**

The checklist on page 184 should help you realize when you need to review your insurance. And there's a list of reliable companies at www.zenvesting.com

Term Versus Whole Life Insurance?

Under no circumstances should you use your life insurance policy as a capital accumulator. You will get a far better return by investing in a pension, a profit-sharing plan, IRA, TSA, 401(k) and the like. A handful of very large insurance companies were severely fined for marketing life insurance policies as investments. **You should only own term life insurance.** Insurance agents will give you many reasons to buy myriad insurance products for estate planning. Don't do it unless a competent fee-only advisor says the use of these policies is absolutely the appropriate strategy based on their understanding of the facts and constraints of your financial situation—and is willing to sign a letter to that effect.

When considering your term insurance policy, try to purchase one that will have the lowest cost over the policy period. In order to maximize your savings, purchase term insurance through a fee-only advisor or directly from a reliable company.

Often, we are dependent on our business partners and it's important to think through what would happen if a partner died. What would your business partner need to survive without you? This is important because your family might need to hold a stake in your business after your death. Generally, that need should be fixed with the cheapest term insurance you can find, since partners in business can change.

See page 188 for a Disability Income Insurance Worksheet.

In general, do not buy life insurance on your children. The primary reason to buy life insurance for children is to provide them with the guaranteed right to buy more insurance when they get older, should they become uninsurable.

You will notice in the life insurance worksheet at the end of this book, that the monthly income is assumed to continue forever to your spouse or children. The reason: if you or your spouse died prematurely, your children would be at an emotional loss and desperately need the time of their surviving parent (who is now a single parent with all the responsibilities of raising a child or children alone). So assume that your husband or wife will need to reduce their work schedule or not work at all until the children become older or go off to college. During that period, they wouldn't be able to save money toward retirement and, therefore, would have to depend on interest from life insurance for life. It is very hard for a fifty- or fifty-five-year-old widowed person to suddenly enter the work-force and try to save enough money for retirement. Life insurance, especially term insurance, is very inexpensive. Have enough to make sure that your family and children are going to have income security for their lifetimes.

See page 186 for Key Disability Contract Provisions.

Beneficiaries

Naturally, any beneficiaries on your insurance policies, investment accounts or retirement plans should be coordinated with your financial planner, lawyer and estate planner. As a general rule, if you are married and do not have a trust set up, you would typically name your spouse as primary beneficiary and your children as secondary beneficiaries. For IRAs and pensions, most planners will tell you to do the same. If your planner or attorney advises otherwise, you should request a signed letter explaining the rationale.

'Welcome home,' nice sentiments but hard if the door of your house has been kicked in, or worse, your house burned and the occupants killed. There is a very strong emotional attachment to a house—to your home and all that it has meant to you. Even after they experience war and persecution one of the things that people who have been forced to leave their village or even their country will say is, 'I just want to go home.'

—CHRISTIAN AID (WWW.CHRISTIAN-AID.ORG).

Protecting Your Livelihood

If you work to support your life, your absolute most important insurance is income protection or what's called disability insurance. Imagine yourself as a money machine and the machine breaks because of sickness or an accident. The effect on your financial security would be tremendous. Thus, it is very important to understand the exact amount your insurance polices would pay if you were ever disabled. Equally important is to understand how your insurance company defines "disabled." A standing joke among insurance agents is that some disability policies are written with such tight restrictions that if you could sell pencils on a street corner you wouldn't get a dime.

The worksheet on page 188 can help you decide how much disability income insurance you will need to support your lifestyle (unless you have extensive personal assets that negate the need for disability insurance), and also help you decide what elimination period you should have on your policy. An elimination period means the number of days you'll have to wait before you receive a benefit from your policy. Generally it runs from a thirty-day to a two-year wait, and the shorter the wait, the more expensive the policy.

I listed the key contract provisions you should have in your policy on page 186. I'd also recommend structuring your policy as an annually renewable graded or step premium policy that keeps your premiums low for years, with premiums gradually increasing. These policies are an excellent buy.

chapter 10

WIDE-AWAKE PARENTING

I believe that if we are to be measured, it should be on our commitments and our ability to fulfill those commitments. As a husband and father, my life's rhythm needs to be in sync with my mate and my children. They are my commitment.—PAUL H. SUTHERLAND

Fear, sloth and apathy are what keep us from giving up the baggage left on our doorstep by our parents. To move on, we must all take a hard look at our inner life, our beliefs about the world and the emotions created by those beliefs. **We must take the time and emotional energy required to re-parent ourselves to a more rational, loving, responsible belief system.** Without this re-parenting, we will continue to react to life's events instead of finding opportunities in difficult situations and the humor in life's ups and downs.

I believe that you can choose to accept your own history and grow from it.

YOU, THE ONE

FROM WHOM ON DIFFERENT PATHS

ALL OF US HAVE COME.

TO WHOM ON DIFFERENT PATHS

ALL OF US ARE GOING.

MAKE STRONG IN OUR

HEARTS WHAT UNITES US.

—BENEDICTINE BROTHER DAVID STEINDL-RAST

Our parents may have taught us differently, but our future and happiness, and the future and happiness of our children, is dependent upon the choices we make in response to life's little-big moments. If we step in dog poop, we have a choice: we can choose to be thankful to be wearing shoes—even if they are new—and laugh out loud at the funny story we have to tell our friends. Or, we can choose to get angry and lash out. Which choice would be a better example for your children?

Mindful parenting simply calls on us to pay attention to what we are doing, including the choices we make, and to examine in an ongoing way the effect our choices have on our child. It involves a continual inquiry into what we are doing and why.—JON AND MYLA KABAT-ZINN, *EVERYDAY BLESSINGS*

Children laugh, on average, up to 300 times a day, adults just seventeen.
—DANIEL NETTLE, *HAPPINESS: THE SCIENCE BEHIND YOUR SMILE*

I've learned that real listening does not require that we come up with answers. Listening itself is the answer.
—JON WILSON, PUBLISHER AND EDITOR OF *HOPE* MAGAZINE

You may think that a life where events—even unpleasant ones—are treated progressively, where anger and frustration melt away in laughter and opportunity, is pure utopia. But that's like asking if we believe in our own best wishes. **The question then becomes, how can we make our own family, our own home, a utopia?**

Utopia in the strict sense of the word, is, by definition, unattainable. But it's worth striving for! How can we expand that vision and make our community, and society as a whole, a utopia? If we don't spend at least some of our time focused on that goal, we allow life to cloud up with negativity.

A Mayonnaise Jar and Two Cups of Coffee

When things in your life seem almost too much to handle, when 24 hours in a day are not enough, remember this story my brother Bob told me about a mayonnaise jar and 2 cups of coffee. A professor stood before his philosophy class with several items in front of him. When the class began, he wordlessly picked up a very large and empty mayonnaise jar and proceeded to fill it with golf balls. He then asked the students if the jar was full. They agreed that it was.

The professor then picked up a box of pebbles and poured them into the jar. He shook the jar lightly and the pebbles rolled into the open areas between the golf balls. He then asked the students again if the jar was full, they agreed it was.

The professor next picked up a box of sand and poured it into the jar. Of course, the sand filled up everything else. He asked once more if the jar was full and the students responded with a unanimous "yes."

The professor then produced two cups of coffee from under the table and poured the entire contents into the jar, effectively filling the empty space between the sand. The students laughed.

"Now," said the professor, as the laughter subsided, "I want you to recognize that this jar represents your life. The golf balls are the important things—your God, your family, your children, your health, your friends, and your favorite passions—things that if everything else was lost and only they remained, your life would still be full.

"The pebbles are the other things that matter, like your job, your house and your car.

"The sand is everything else—the small stuff.

"If you put the sand into the jar first," he continued, "there is no room for the pebbles or the golf balls. The same goes for life. If you spend all your time and energy on the small stuff, you will never have room for the things that are important to you. Pay attention to the things that are critical to your happiness. Play with your children. Take time to get medical checkups. Take your partner out to dinner. Play another 18. There will always be time to clean the house and fix the disposal. Take care of the golf balls first—the things that really matter. Set your priorities. The rest is just sand."

One of the students raised her hand and inquired what the coffee represented.

The professor smiled. "I'm glad you asked. It just goes to show you that no matter how full your life may seem, there's always room for a couple of cups of coffee with a friend."

Teaching Kids about Money

> Amos: "Kingfish, where'd you get your good judgment?"
> Kingfish: "From my experience."
> Amos: "And where'd you get your experience?"
> Kingfish: "From bad judgment."
> —FROM THE AMOS 'N' ANDY TV SHOW

Most of what our children will learn about money comes from the way we, as their parents, manage our time and money. Before I had children of my own, I felt like I had true insights and understanding and was positive about the ideal way to teach children about financial responsibility. Now, I understand that teaching children about money management is much like teaching them about happiness, responsibility, how to get along with others, how to make decisions, how to feel good about themselves and how to be kind. In other words, it is done mostly by example in small bits everyday.

Learning by example is something that children do automatically, all the time; so when it comes to money, be aware of your attitudes and how they might affect your children's views. **If you want your children to enjoy work and get excited about going to college** then you'd better reflect joy, passion and happiness in your own work. If you come home and complain about how you work your rear-end off, unappreciated by your family, clients, employees or employer, despite, of course, all the wonderful things that you do for them, your children are bound to reflect your frustration and lack of balance in life. They may grow up thinking that work is all about drudgery, not passion. They may decide that work is a curse and burden of adulthood, not the blessing of being able to discover, express, serve and produce creatively.

Children also need to learn about the relationship between time and money. For example, when my children ask me why we don't live in a giant house, I point out that we have a nice house, and that to have a "giant" house I would have to work more hours or give less to charities. I tell them I'd rather spend more time traveling with them, helping others, being outdoors or playing board games together than working for a bigger house.

Possessions are power in our society. A child who feels lost or powerless can easily turn to objects, thinking that they will make him feel better. The development of a child's inner life, his sense of himself and his own unique being, requires something more complex than the latest 'cool' sneakers. Helping our children find soul-feeding activities—whether martial arts, dance, sports, playing a musical instrument, backpacking, drawing, fixing or building things, journal writing, singing or rapping, or whatever speaks to who they are—is a needed balance to the quick fixes of our consumer-oriented culture.
—JON AND MYLA KABAT-ZINN, *EVERYDAY BLESSINGS*

Learning to spend money wisely is also a good lesson. My thirteen year old son Keeston often asks why we can't have a fast, fancy boat. Instead of just answering him by saying, "It's too much money," I point out that a boat takes up a lot of time. Boat owners have to worry about where to rent a slip and how to keep the boat in repair. I tell them that in the summer I want us to spend time together on the beach, or hiking, or playing tennis. If we had a fancy boat we might feel obligated to use it every time we were free. If we need a boat, I can also point out, we can always rent one. Kids who are old enough to ask for big boats or big houses are also old enough to appreciate this kind of reasoning.

The pleasures, the values of contact with the natural world, are not reserved for the scientists. They are available to anyone who will place himself under the influence of a lonely mountain top—or the sea—or the stillness of a forest; or who will stop to think about so small a thing as the mystery of a growing seed.—RACHEL CARSON, *LOST WOODS: THE DISCOVERED WRITING OF RACHEL CARSON* BY RACHEL CARSON AND LINDA LEAR

Karl Fisch is the author of *The Fischbowl*, a staff development blog for Arapahoe High School teachers exploring constructivism and 21st century learning skills. http://thefischbowl.blogspot.com/

Kids, Money and the Real World

It's good to have discussions about money with your kids, but it's also necessary to pass practical skills onto them that will be of use out in the world, and there are a plenty of opportunities. A good one is at sit-down restaurants. Ever since my kids could compute percentages, I have had them figure out the server's tip on our bill. They can help decide whether or not we received good service, and whether the server earned a ten or a twenty percent tip. A cheerful, helpful waiter or waitress can affect the overall enjoyment of a meal out, and this can also show my kids that rewards come from doing a good job.

When we stay at hotels, sometimes we are having so much fun swimming that I let the kids order meals poolside. I have them read the menu and the prices, and often they will say something like, "Daddy, the grilled cheese at the snack bar is $5, and on this menu its $9! But we think it's worth the extra $4 to just sit here by the pool." They like the fun they have swimming. I like that they are learning about the value of money.

Then there's the food court. Often, before seeing a movie at our local theater in the mall, the kids and I go there for a bite to eat. My daughter always wants to go to Subway or Taco Bell, while my son usually wants Chinese food. I give each of them cash to pay for their order. I always give them the largest bills in my wallet. My young son and daughter often come back with change from a $100 bill plus their bean burrito or noodles. I've been doing this since they were four or five years old, and they've always responded in the same ways. My daughter will count the money back to me exactly, while my son will just put the bills and change on the tray, uncounted and often in disarray. Sometimes I'll ask my

son to count it to ensure that the cashier did not make a mistake. Giving your children opportunities to use money also gives you, the parent, a chance to see where they might need extra help in the future.

Kids and Your Home Purchase

Nowhere are our values more in evidence than in the homes we choose to live in with our families. Ever since becoming a father, I have brought my children with me to the closing on a new house and had them look through the financial documents with me. Even though they may have initially had little conception of the big numbers involved in such a large purchase, I wanted them to feel comfortable in offices and conference rooms. I wanted them to feel comfortable watching, and someday participating in, a live financial transaction. Before the closing, I always ask the realtor to make up special forms for my children to sign. When we are through, I have them sign those documents to make our house purchase official to them. The house is theirs too, after all: it will be their home.

We are currently preparing students for jobs that don't exist …
Using technologies that have not yet been invented … In order to solve
problems that we don't even know are problems yet.—KARL FISCH

Kids and Chores

My children are expected to help with household chores; I do not believe it is appropriate to pay children to do household chores. An exception would be specific "jobs" like mowing lawns or cleaning the garage. Although Amy and I are experimenting with a plan to tie allowance to behavior, as a way of establishing good habits and rewarding behaviors we appreciate, I do believe that children should do household chores because they are part of the family. Whether it is taking out the garbage, putting groceries away, helping clean up dinner dishes or folding laundry, they do these tasks to help keep the household running smoothly and not for economic benefit.

To get paid for everything creates a system where the children think everything must have a monetary value. It teaches children to "keep score" rather than help out. Creating this kind of transactional relationship with a child at a young age teaches them to be transactional in adulthood, which can lead to very unhealthy relationships with romantic partners and friends. Life should be about love, not about keeping score.

Allowances

Most of us, as children, spent our allowance money on toys or candy. It's easy to continue that "spend it now" pattern into adulthood, and wind up with uncontrollable debt. As a father, I want my children to understand that money is not just to buy toys. It is also to pay for living expenses, save for the future and help people who need help. Most of the time, I think my children understand that.

For monthly allowances, my thirteen-year-old gets $75. To begin to teach him the art of budgeting, he gets $25 payable to him titled "Long Term Savings" (which goes into his investment and savings accounts), $25 titled "Charity" with the payee on the check left blank and $25 for himself.

When my daughter turned sixteen, I decided that she was ready to learn to budget on her own. To work out her allowance, I sat down with her and we figured out how much was spent each month on school expenses, clothing, shampoo, haircuts, social events and car expenses, as well as ten percent each for charity and savings. In order for my daughter to earn her allowance, I made our expectations for school grades, volunteer work, extra curricular activities, school sports and activities and part-time summer work clear to her. She created envelopes for each budget category, then took her monthly allowance and divided it up among the different categories. It is interesting that she tends to save more and spend less than we thought on clothing and entertainment. In the summer she works so her allowance is all put into her investment and savings accounts for use when she goes to college.

Money rules our lives. You can say it doesn't. You can rail against it. You can claim to be above it or indifferent to it. You can do all the moral and intellectual gymnastics that you will. But when all is said and done, money is at the center of our very claim to existence. Yet money is not of central importance. It has nothing what-soever to do with the lasting values that make life worth living. There, in a nutshell, is the dilemma. How do you reconcile yourself to something that is not important but is at the very center of your life?

—KENT NERBURN, *LETTERS TO MY SON: REFLECTIONS ON BECOMING A MAN*

Lessons on gambling

As children grow and begin to have bigger "wants," not just needs, the idea of free passes, or free money, can become very attractive. We happen to live in a state where there are casinos, and for some people, early exposure to these can grow into gambling problems later in life. Winning the slot machine on your first, youthful trip to the casino might make you subconsciously believe that you're destined to win every time you play.

To arm your children against accepting this fallacy, stress to them that gambling is for entertainment, not income. On a recent trip to Las Vegas, my children's mother and her husband made sure the children understood they were going to the casino to have fun—not to get rich by gambling. They showed the kids the math: their mom won $200, which, as explained to me by my daughter Akasha, was much less than offset by what had been spent on the hotel room, the plane ticket, and meals. At the end of this equation, the kids understand, "It's just for fun."

I do not know what I may appear to the world; but to myself I seem to have been only like a boy playing on the seashore, and diverting myself in now and then finding a smoother pebble or a prettier shell than ordinary, whilst the great ocean of truth lay all undiscovered before me.

—ISAAC NEWTON

hapter 11

KIDS & EDUCATION

*Perhaps the most valuable result of all education is the ability to make yourself
do the thing you have to do, when it ought to be done, whether you like it or
not; it is the first lesson that ought to be learned; and however early a man's
training begins, it is probably the last lesson that he learns thoroughly.*
—THOMAS H. HUXLEY

Wisdom is priceless! If you are two, ten, eighteen, fifty, or even eighty, education is your best investment. Education champions knowledge, curiosity, creativity, assertiveness, debate, reading, exploring, helpfulness and compassion. Education highlights heroes, doers, tryers and happy, hopeful people. The education can be formal, it can be through apprenticeship or by the do-it-yourself method; no matter how, education brings security to families and society.

The best place to teach children about education is at home. As with money management, you are teaching your children about the importance of education through your example. If you want your kids to succeed in life and be happy, well-adjusted, good citizens, then raise them in a culture of education from conception. A loving and accepting home-life combined with stimulating playful schools will encourage a love and appreciation of learning. Sending a kid to college is easy; fostering an education culture takes real commitment.

The Absolute, 100%, No Risk, Guaranteed Best Investment. Anyone in the United States can get a great education if they will put in the effort, show up on time and apply themselves.

That is not to say that having money for college isn't important. We all know that it is. But there are options: you and your son or daughter can apply for scholarships, grants and loans. A part-time job could supplement money saved for college. If there is no college fund, there are other opportunities—full-time jobs and night school, or taking six years to complete four years of college while working. Just let your child know ahead of time what you can provide and what's expected of them. Honestly, the best thing a parent can do is feed their child's natural curiosity and nurture a love of education.

The Scoop on the 529 Plan

College not only teaches specific skills, it gives your children tools to communicate and persuade among peers, and to adapt and thrive to a constantly changing environment. These are abilities that they will use virtually every day of their lives, in work and at home. So what's college worth? Well, statistically, a college graduate will make $1,000,000 more over his or her lifetime than a person who has only completed high school. So make sure your child knows that a college education will earn them a million dollars. That will motivate them to excel in high school.

For parents who wish to save for college, I recommend they first concentrate on building their net worth. Fully fund 403(b), 401(k)s, IRAs and other tax qualified retirement plans. They are the best way to accumulate money even if they are cashed out to pay for college. Setting aside money in a College Savings Plan should come after your tax-qualified 401(k), IRAs, 403(b) or other retirement plan contributions. Even if you must partially cash in your retirement plans or borrow against them, you will most likely be ahead over funding a 529 Plan.

Why is that? Let's say you only have $1,000 in your budget for education. That would be equivalent to a $1,500 pre-tax contribution in an IRA, 401(k), or 403(b) qualified plan (if you're in the 35% tax bracket). If you add another $1,500 annually for ten years, your money will grow to $20,500 from those deposits, assuming a 6% return. That compares to the $1,000 (after taxes) that you could give annually to a 529 Plan, which would grow to $13,650 in ten years. As mentioned earlier, when your children begin college you'll have the option of stopping all or part of your deposits to the retirement plan in order to fund college, freeing up about $1,000 a year towards tuition. You can also borrow or cash in on the retirement plan. Any of these options places you ahead of having funded a 529 Plan or other non-tax deductible option to fund college.

For an up-to-date list of 529 Plans and other investment options, plus a state-by-state comparison tool, go to www.zenvesting.com, and view the links under "Education."

Once your tax qualified plans are funded, the 529 Plan is a great option that allows you to make contributions to your child's future tuition needs. One of the major benefits of the 529 Plan is the power of the compounded investment return realized because the assets grow tax-free until the funds are needed for college. In addition to being able to make tax-free withdrawals to meet qualified higher education expenses, some states offer an immediate state tax deduction for contributions made to an in-state 529 Plan. (Note that tax-free withdrawals are currently set to expire after 2010.) In addition to the tax-free withdrawals, some states offer matching contributions as an effort to stimulate participation.

Each state has adopted at least one 529 Plan, and investors have flexibility in investing in either their own state's 529 Plan or an out-of-state plan. However, it should be noted that Morningstar has listed the following states offer plans with excessive fees and poor choices of investments: Maine, Arizona, Pennsylvania, Nebraska and Ohio. Among the best were the Michigan Education Savings Program, Virginia's College America and the Minnesota College Savings Plan.

Under most 529 Plans, you are able to contribute to each beneficiary, without affecting your taxes, up to $12,000 a year. In 2005, the government also bestowed the ability to "front-end load" the investment plan with $60,000 per beneficiary in one year. However, you will not be able to make any additional contributions or other gifts for the same beneficiary for five years unless you use some of your unified estate-tax credit. The maximum contributions that can be made for one beneficiary over their lifetime range from $100,000 to $235,000, depending upon your individual state plan. You should consult with your fee-only financial planner, accountant or CPA to determine if you wish to exceed the $12,000 annual or $60,000 one-time limit.

Compared with a UGMA (Uniform Gifts to Minors Act) custodial account, the 529 Plan offers more control over your assets since even at the age of majority (18 or 21 in most states) the child does not have legal title. This means that as the account holder, you can change the beneficiary of the plan to another child, your spouse or even yourself if issues arise and the original beneficiary does not elect to further their education. Also, even though you maintain control over the use of the funds in the plan, the assets are out of your taxable estate if you were to suffer a premature death.

University Of Pennsylvania, Class of 2008

Finance 101 for Your College-Age Kid
By Kristen Patton

Establish a monthly budget. Plan out estimated expenses for each month, including a small amount for the unexpected. This may require adjustments during the first few months, but afterwards it should remain relatively uniform. Of course emergencies sometimes arise, but otherwise the budget should be followed.

Beware of the debit card. It's a favorite tool of college students everywhere: almost as liquid as cash, but without the hassle. While it is convenient and practical, it's also easy to lose track of small purchases; those five-dollar lattes during late night study sessions really add up after a few weeks.

Encourage your child to keep track of their checking account balance. It's shocking how many college students have no idea how much money they have, and many overdraw their accounts frequently. Students should write down all checks written, ATM withdrawals, and debit purchases. This will give your child an idea of how much money they are actually spending and help them stay in line with their budget. This is a good habit for people of all ages; it allows you to double check your balance and recognize any fraudulent spending taking place on your account.

Make your child accountable for credit card purchases. Giving your child a credit card in their name is a good way to help them establish their credit for later in life. However, if the bill is sent home, it should be used sparingly, for purchases such as books, plane tickets home, academic fees, or emergency situations. Everyday expenses should come out of the established budget, and therefore should not be charged. Look over the bill and ask questions before you pay it each month.

Make your child responsible for a portion of their tuition. Most financial aid packages include an expected student contribution, and there is no reason why your student shouldn't actually pay this money! Some combination of summer earnings and a job during the academic year should be able to cover this amount. If your child does not have a financial aid package, then your family can decide together what a reasonable contribution is for your student.

Help your child prioritize their activities. If your student chooses to participate in expensive extracurriculars, such as Greek life or a club sport, then something else may have to go. Also, such activities should not be the reason that your student doesn't have time for a job.

Make your child work for special trips. You know that in the real world you must save money in advance for vacations. Don't let your child throw last minute spring break expenses on you. If a special opportunity has expenses that would be unreasonable for your child to pay, give them an amount to work towards (you pay for the plane ticket, I'll pay for your living expenses, etc.).

Don't keep your child in the dark about their expenses. They should know how much their tuition, transportation costs, room and board, and meal plan cost. Sometimes students are unaware of how many expenses besides tuition come with college. Knowing the actual amount will give them some perspective on the importance of this investment.

Remember that your "child" is an adult. Most undergraduate college students are between the ages of 18 and 22. They are old enough to understand that money must be earned, and they should be able to handle their expenses without you holding their hand. They should learn to be respectful of and grateful for your contribution to their education and be willing to make some of their own sacrifices in order to help out.

Never doubt that a small group of committed people can change the world. Indeed, it is the only thing that ever has. —MARGARET MEAD

SUDDENLY RICH...OR NOT

All booms are the same: they make me nervous. They're hard places in which to find bargains, and I can never get the fact out of my head that: Every boom contains the seeds of the next bust.
—MARK MOBIUS, WITH STEPHEN FENICHELL, *PASSPORT TO PROFITS*

Aha! You're reading this chapter first because you just won the lottery, got a divorce windfall, earned a giant buyout from your company, sold your business for a profit, inherited Great-Aunt Louisa's estate or a simple act of kindness unexpectedly garnered you a grateful reward. Regardless, you have "gobs" of money, so what should you do?

First, go back, start at the beginning and read this book cover to cover. You owe it to yourself to get "smart" about money and finances. Like I've said, education is **The Absolute, 100%, No Risk, Guaranteed Best Investment.**

Back again? Here are some quick, no frills suggestions:

Put the money safely in CD's, Treasury bills, or a high-interest money market fund while you figure out your game plan.

Do not immediately say "Yes," to anyone's request for money!

Get good solid advice from fee-only advisors who are used to working with wealthy people. See a CPA to learn about taxes for your new financial status, an attorney to understand your new estate and discuss wills and the like, and a fee-only financial planner (a NAPFA member would be my advice, but not all NAPFA members are alike). It's important to find advisors that already work with wealthy families; their experience will serve and protect your new wealth.

So I'm rich now! Why aren't I happy? Why do I worry? Why do I feel embarrassed? What if I make a mistake? Will people like me for "me" or because I am rich? All these questions might flow through your head and can be unsettling. **Seek out a therapist, rabbi, minister, monk, priest or whoever you might feel comfortable with**, who has counseling education and experience to help you address these feelings.

Be confidential. Imagine if a friend called and said, "I just received $100,000,000!" Would you see them in the same light? Heck no! Be honest. The freedom and power money provides changes people's behavior and attitudes completely.

*Therefore, the True Person governs by emptying the heart of desire
and filling the belly with food, weakening ambitions and strengthening bones.
If the people are simple and free from desire, then the clever ones never dare
to interfere. Practice action without striving and all will be in order.*
—TAO TE CHING

$36 and the Lottery

Statistically the average lottery ticket buyer has a lower than average income
and spends $36 a month proving that they failed math at school. If they took
that $36 every month and put it away, here is what they could expect.

$36/Month

	5 years	10 years	15 years	20 years	25 years	30 years
6%	$2,511	$5,899	$10,469	$16,633	$24,947	$36,162
8%	$2,645	$6,586	$12,457	$21,204	$34,236	$53,652
10%	$2,787	$7,374	$14,920	$27,337	$47,766	$81,377

**The financially rich people you know are smart—they saved and invested
wisely to let the magic of compounding work for them.**

*It is not the strongest of the species that survives, nor the most intelligent,
but the one most responsive to change.*—CHARLES DARWIN

Chapter 13

UTOPIAN RETIREMENT—
SIX STEPS TO CALCULATE
WHAT YOU'LL NEED

Retirement Is Not For Sissies
—SEEN ON A BUMPERSTICKER

Don't retire. Retirement is awful. You won't like it. Keep working for the rest of your life. Retirement's charms are oversold and plain no fun. Many people are in retirement and hate it! Why? They didn't prepare themselves for it.

What is Retirement?

Retirement means working
If you want to
When you want to
Where you want to
How you want to
Forever

That's right. Forever.
In retirement, you must plan to live forever.

This cannot be stressed enough. Many retirees of this millennium will live another forty to seventy years than the current generation thanks to healthy lifestyles and modern medicine. Can you imagine having a retirement life longer than your working life? And if you can imagine it, will you have enough resources to sustain your lifestyle?

Planning for Your Retirement Means Planning for Your Retirement

Planning for a secure retirement takes a certain amount of hope and faith, as well as the proper tools. To give your retirement wings, you must take steps now. It's that simple. In the words of Roman statesman and philosopher, Marcus Cicero, "As you sow, so shall you reap." Perhaps the phrase sounds familiar because it's found verbatim in both the New and Old Testaments of the Bible, while the Koran asks the question, "Have you considered what you sow?" And there's a good reason these words have been passed down from generation to generation: as personal development author Chuck Gallozzi says, As you sow, so shall you reap is "an immutable law of nature with as much force as the law of gravity."

Naturally, the devil is in the details. Retiring with security requires a consistent savings schedule and the knowledge to use retirement planning and investment tools wisely. But, as the Taoists say, **a journey of a thousand miles begins with a single step.**

Step One—Imagine It

Fear about how one will support oneself in the future arises not because there is no way of sustaining oneself, but because one's mind is poor.—JAE WOONG KIM, *POLISHING THE DIAMOND, ENLIGHTENING THE MIND*

The first step we'll take is an exercise in visualization. Pause and imagine your first day of retirement. Will you be packing for a trip? Will you spend the day looking for a new home? Will you go for a long walk? Play tennis with a friend? Begin a long book? Plan a dinner party? A weekend kayaking?

If you're planning the dinner party or that kayaking adventure, what will you do with the rest of your week? How about the week after your party and your trip? And the week after that? And the week after that? How many weeks are there in a year?

See what I mean about forever.

Think big: travel, education, a new career. Do you want to spend several months of your retirement years traveling? Will your life be full of holidays? The word holiday is derived from "holy" day—will each of your retirement days be a holy day? Do you imagine yourself working part-time, not so much for the money, but for the feeling of worth you get from helping others? Will you live in two different places, or two different countries?

Of course, there is no right or wrong answer for what a proper retirement vision is. The only thing that is essential is that you go into retirement with an attitude of "here's what I think I'm going to do, but I'm open to different possibilities." Statistics show that if you believe that life—physically, mentally, and emotionally—ends at retirement or starts its decline at retirement, then that's what is in store for you. Statistics also state, however, that retirees who have healthy lifestyles, keep mentally and emotionally fit, maintain supportive relationships, have future plans and have financial security, can actually experience an increase in their health after they retire. The point is that a wonderful, robust, joyful retirement is completely dependent on you and your behaviors.

We shall not cease from exploration
And the end of all our exploring
Will be to arrive where we started
And know the place for the first time. —T.S. ELIOT, "LITTLE GIDDING"

Step Two—Rich, Healthy & Wise

It's time to sit down with your spouse or significant other plus some pencils and paper. Together, dream up the most outrageously blissful retirement ideas. **Write it all down—every fantasy, whim, every out-there excursion.**

Now, set it aside for a while, discuss it a bit; notice how the wild plans start to solidify into a more permanent (and realizable) image. The reality is that your retirement adventure will change over time just like your fantasies and your dreams. Often retirees (don't you hate that word?) will find that their lives are very busy and full of activity early in their retirement; later, this dizziness wanes until a happy medium is reached. I have noticed a pretty even split between clients who engage in very busy early retirement years, slowing down as they get older, spending more time with children, close friends, a good book, surfing the internet and other more passive activities, and the other half who become much busier over time. One eighty-three-year-old client reported, "My wife isn't happy unless we always have three different vacations planned, scheduled, and paid for."

Retirement lasts a long time, but it doesn't feel that way psychologically because as we age, time shrinks. When you were ten years old, one year was one-tenth of your life; when you are seventy, that year is only one-seventieth of your life. It will feel like it passes seven times faster than the years of your youth. Realize when filling out the upcoming worksheets that you will have ample time, and that time will have a different meaning to you than it has in the past, both because you're older and more understanding, and because each day in retirement will seem shorter. Thus, if your desire is to travel in retirement, plan on your trips being longer, more leisurely and less hectic than the trips you take today. Some people are old at thirty, others remain young at ninety. Not to belabor this point, but **if you think you'll be old at seventy, then you can count on being old at seventy.**

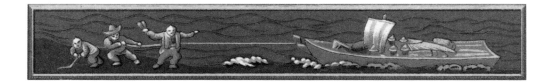

Time for Money Worksheet

I/we would like to trade less time for money at or around age ___.

I/we would like it to be unnecessary to trade time for money at or around age ___.

Describe your retirement, housing and travel dreams. Who will live with you?

Do you want to be near relatives and friends?

Describe your ideal living situation here:

Let's say you just retired and your doctor tells you,
"I have good news and bad news—which do you want first?"
You say, "I want the good news first."
He tells you, "You have 3 years to live!"
You say, "That's the good news?"
He replies, "Yes, because I forgot to tell you a year ago!"

I have often found that the first year or so of retirement can foretell the "look" of a client's remaining life pattern. I want you to really think about what you'd do if you had to cram it all into two years. How will you live? Who will you want to hang out with? What do you want to see? How will you want to be remembered? (Make sure that both partners in the marriage or relationship write down their plans.)

Now imagine that a higher power comes to you a few days later and says, "Your doctor made a mistake! You will live to age one hundred as sound-minded, healthy, vital and energetic as you are today. You can climb mountains, take tantra courses, go on a hiking trip with your grandkids, build your own cabin, work as a volunteer teaching sports to kids in Namibia or take up scuba diving. Also don't worry if you want to go back to school to get a Ph.D. in peace studies, your brain and mental stamina will be better than it has ever been."

What do you want your retirement to look like?

These exercises should have given you a chance to think about what you really want out of life after you're done trading time for money.

_____

_____

_____

_____

_____

_____

_____

_____

_____

_____

Caution: Budget Busters

From my experience, the main budget buster in retirement is the needs and wants of children and grandchildren. This worksheet provides a little wiggle room to help ensure that you can stay retired and within your budget should unforeseen expenses come up. However, be aware that if you have trouble saying no to your children before retirement, you'll have trouble saying no after retirement.

Another issue that can make the best laid plans go awry is the once-in-a-lifetime vacation to celebrate retirement. It is essential to distinguish between what is considered a vacation and what is "normal" retirement travel. For example, one of my successfully retired clients and his wife spend three months a year at their cottage on an island in northern Michigan, one month at a condo time share in the Caribbean, and a fair amount of the balance of the year at their real (so to speak, especially for tax purposes) home in Nevada. They do not consider the time spent in Michigan or the Caribbean as vacations but rather as part of their retirement lifestyle, so this "normal travel" is calculated into their annual budget. I'm not dissuading you from that blow-out dream vacation, but it would need to be a special addendum to the annual budget.

Never put a period where God has put a comma.

—GRACIE ALLEN QUOTED IN THE UNITED CHURCH OF CHRIST'S *GOD IS STILL SPEAKING* CAMPAIGN

Step Three: It's About Money: Turn Your Retirement Vision Into Numbers

Here's where we quantify your retirement income needs. What does your fantasy retirement cost in today's dollars?

Don't sweat the small stuff. It doesn't matter if the fantasy budget and the visioning statement changes many times between now and retirement. That's fine and as normal as can be. These numbers will all tend to be pretty rough, so it's best to be more conservative. You also want to have a margin of error in your budget; after you're done, increase the total by an extra twenty to thirty percent. This budget surplus will give you greater financial security and also more flexibility.

Also, don't fret about inflation or deflation when completing this part of the retirement worksheet. In other words, we won't talk about gas costing $10 a gallon or cars $100,000. Use numbers as if you were retiring today. It is your portfolio's job to ensure that you'll have enough at retirement. Simply be as reasonable and exact as you can.

Time For Money Retirement Budget Worksheet

This exercise should be done with your spouse or significant other.

	Annual Estimate	**Monthly**
Home maintenance (est. 2% of value) (plus mortg. payment, if any)	$_____ / 12 =	_____
Second Home Maintenance (2% of value) (plus mortg. payment, if any)	$_____ / 12 = $_____ / 12 =	_____ _____
Travel/Vacations	$_____ / 12 =	_____
Home Insurance	$_____ / 12 =	_____
Property Taxes	$_____ / 12 =	_____
Car Payments*	$_____ / 12 =	_____
Auto Expenses (Maintenance and gas)	$_____ / 12 =	_____
Clothing	$_____ / 12 =	_____
Communication (Phone, cell phone, cable service, computer)	$_____ / 12 =	_____
Utilities (Electric/gas/garbage/water)	$_____ / 12 =	_____
Groceries/Vitamins	$_____ / 12 =	_____
Entertainment (Dvds, movies, theater, eating out, CDs, sports events, concerts)	$_____ / 12 =	_____

* Usually you pay cash for cars in retirement so you have reverse payments—you budget that you'll buy a car every three to ten years. Thus, if you'll spend $30,000 on a car every 5 years you'll need to budget $6,000 annually or $500 a month for car payments.

Education/Personal Development $_____ / 12 = _____
   (Classes, lectures, books, e-courses,
   seminars, magazine subscriptions)

Sundries (toiletries, cosmetics, etc.) $_____ / 12 = _____

Sanity $_____ / 12 = _____
   (yoga, counseling, sports, clubs)

Fun $_____ / 12 = _____
   (wine, wine tastings, lattés)

Tithing (religious) $_____ / 12 = _____

Charitable Contributions $_____ / 12 = _____
   (budgeted amount)

Insurance/Healthcare Costs $_____ / 12 = _____
   (usually $700 to $2500 per person,
   per month)

Children/Grandchildren $_____ / 12 = _____
   (Gifts, graduation, loans)

Helping Others (usually lump sum gifts) $_____ / 12 = _____

Christmas/Anniversary/Birthday Gifts $_____ / 12 = _____

_____ $_____ / 12 = _____

_____ $_____ / 12 = _____

Total annual/monthly
expenses estimated $_____ / 12 = _____

Plus 65% of above to estimate expenses $_____ / 12 = _____
   (for taxes and margin of error)

**Equals total annual/monthly
expenses estimate** $_____ / 12 = _____

Step Four: Estimate Income from Other Sources

In order to project your income from other sources, you will need to estimate your Social Security payments. **Never assume, however, that Social Security will provide more than one-fourth of your income,** just in case the program is not completely solvent. In retirement planning, look at Social Security income as gravy.

If you or your spouse qualifies for a fixed pension, naturally this income should be added to and considered (a place is given in the Step Four Worksheet). Estimate the pension income assuming a Joint and 100 Percent Survivor benefit. Do not assume anything else unless you are working with a competent fee-only retirement planner, with ten years or more experience.

Estimated Social Security Income

Use the figures below as a guide. If both you and your spouse or partner work and earn over $50,000 each, the estimates on the left apply to both; if just one works, the estimates on the right apply to the second spouse (half of the working partner's income).

For Each Working Spouse or Partner Estimate	**For A Non-Working Partner Estimate:**
Retired at 50 = $9,000	Retired at 50 = $4,500
Retired at 55 = $10,000	Retired at 55 = $5,000
Retired at 60 = $12,000	Retired at 60 = $6,000
Retired at 65 = $18,000	Retired at 65 = $9,000

Total Social Security Estimated (Annual Income) $_____

Next, by calculating your estimated income from other sources, you can find the annual or monthly income you will need in order to retire. Start with the number you ended up in the Time For Money Worksheet on page 130:

Estimated Income From Other Sources

Estimate of total income needs (annual or monthly figure): $_____
   (from last line of the Time For Worksheet)

Less estimated Social Security: $_____

Less income from fixed pension (if any): $_____

**Equals total annual or monthly income needed from $_____
   investment portfolio**

This number will be used to calculate how much money, including all retirement funds and assets, you will need to save in order to reach your retirement goals.

Step Five: How Much Will I Need?

In this Step, you'll be turning the total income needed from your investment portfolio you calculated in Worksheet Four into the lump sum dollar amount you will need to have saved when you stop working. What we're looking for is "the number," as some people put it. What's your retirement number? How much cash do you need in savings and portfolios so that you can live out your retirement fantasies and visions?

First, we need to determine your risk tolerance. If you're conservative, then you'll want to assume that you can draw about three and one-half percent from your portfolio. This will mean that you're going to get about $36,000 for every million dollars that you have in savings. If you have more of a long-term orientation or can retire at an older age, then you're can assume a more aggressive income of six percent, or about $50,000 per million dollars saved. If you fall somewhere in between, or if you are not sure, just assume you are a balanced or yield investor with a portfolio yield of about four and a quarter percent. Since everybody's different, you will have to decide what works best for your particular situation.

If you're a(n)	Percentage to Withdraw Annually	Percentage to Withdraw Monthly	$1 Million = Income of	
			annually	monthly
Aggressive Investor	6	0.05	$60,000	$5000
Balanced Investor	5.4	0.045	$54,000	$4500
Yield Income Investor	4.8	0.04	$48,000	$4000
Capital Preservation	3.6	0.03	$36,000	$3000

Next, calculate your retirement "number." Use the annual percentage to withdraw (PTW) rate you chose above for this equation.

Worksheet: How Much Will I Need?

Annual income needed: $_____ / PTW rate_____% = "Number" $_____
  (Note: The PTW rate should be 3%, 4% or 6%)

This is your "number" and gives you the lump sum you need to retire.

Use these strategies only under the advice of an experienced, fee-only advisor who agrees that these rates are consistent with your needs and risk tolerance.

All of these worksheets (with built-in calculators) are available for you at www.zenvesting.com.

In the next step, you will use this number to calculate how much money is necessary to save in order to reach your retirement goals. Also, you'll be able to quickly see, using the Lump Sum Retirement Saving method, whether you will be able to reach your goals.

Step Six: How Much Do I Need To Save?

First, let's look again at your assets and security. If you are going to have a home mortgage, and you will be living in the home, you must make sure you have calculated that when creating your annual budget. Should you plan to sell your present home upon retirement, to downsize or to travel, that needs to be factored in here as well.

Next, we'll also want to make sure that you'll have some extra security in retirement, so in addition to your budget, you should create an emergency fund or easily liquidated assets that are earmarked especially for unexpected occasions. It is best to have money set aside to cover six months of yearly financial requirements. For example, if you had budgeted $50,000 annually, then your emergency funds or assets would be worth $25,000.

Finally, it's a good idea to be completely debt-free at retirement. But if you anticipate that won't be the case, then you should include the lump sum needed to cover the debts and add it to the retirement sum. It's okay to have debts at retirement—there actually can be advantages to it via tax savings—but in order to make your projections work we must turn those various debts into a lump sum number.

Lump Sum Retirement Saving Worksheet

A) First, write down "the number" from the last worksheet. $_____
    Add any remaining mortgage you will have at retirement. $_____
    Also add your six month cushion (annual income/2). $_____
    Lump Sum Needed $_____

B) Now, have a look at all of your assets that you've already saved for your retire-
    ment. Add together all of your current balances in your 401(k)s, IRAs, personal
    savings, and investment real estate holdings. $_____

C) Subtract the above number from your Lump Sum Needed;
    this is your **Total Lump Sum** needed to save before you retire: $_____

    This is the amount you will be able to save before you can retire. How close is
    this sum to the Total Lump Sum Needed? If it's greater, then you might be able
    to retire earlier. If it is less, you should think about saving more, saving longer,
    or both.

D) The easy way to do all these calculations is to go to www.zenvesting.com as
    the magic of compounding returns will be done automatically for you. We will
    use one return assumption for *The Virtue of Wealth* book. A good investing
    goal is to best inflation by 6%. So we will use 6% for our return assumption to
    help you get a good "how much do I need to save" number.

See Present Value and Future Value tables
at www.zenvesting.com to help you
make these calculations.

How much will my current resources provide?

Lump sum amount you currently have to invest (401(k), IRA's, etc.) = _____
  (if "0" go to next step)

_____ Lump sum x Factor _____   = $_____
  (which is the amount you'll have if you save no more.)

E)   Your lump sum $ needed $_____
     (from A)

Amount you'll have if your current investments grow at 6%   - $_____

Amount you'll need to accumulate in savings   = $_____

How much do I need to save?

Amount I need to accumulate in savings $_____

Lump sum_____/(divided) factor before = _____monthly savings

Is the monthly amount needed to save more than you can afford? Read the next
chapter then come back to this chapter. Look to retire later on, reduce your "wants"
if you still are a ways away from your goal. At www.zenvesting.com all this is easy
to do with our calculators.

How Much for How Much?

The amount of money you will need to provide you with lifetime income security will depend upon several soft assumptions. First your amassed investment portfolio returns are drawing a number that we know will be inaccurate. However, we can use history to help us and we need to do something, so for the purpose of direction here are the assumptions to make.

If you are an investor that can stand a lot of volatility, understand that investment markets will go up and down, and are flexible and global in your approach, then 6% can be a reasonable draw on your portfolio. We will assume you're full of common sense by the time you start investing your retirement nest egg, or that you completely delegate to a solid, ethics investment advisor with a good, long track record.

Business persons, risk takers, and global equity income investors need $100,000 for each $12,000 of annual income, assuming 6% withdrawal. Capital preservation CD, money markets, and short term bond investors need $400,000 for each $12,000 annual income assuming 3% withdrawal.

Note: The business person, global equity investor should be able to handle a portfolio with volatility of 20% to 35%. The CD, money market investor less than 5%. Most investors will fall in the middle of the road. You might assume you'll need $300,000 for each $12,000 of annual income assuming 4% withdrawal.

Oh, and invest like there's no finish line. But that's the next chapter.

chapter 14

FAST-FORWARD RETIREMENT

Do one thing every day that scares you.—ELEANOR ROOSEVELT

Believe it or not, you can live like a king or a queen on just a Social Security check in more than half of the countries in the world. Right here in the US, you can live well by purchasing a smaller house, entertaining more at home than in restaurants, buying quality instead of quantity. The bottom line is you can quick-time your way to your freedom number—it all has to do with the choices you make. Some of these choices are big and easy, like owning a more humble car. Some are small and steady, like turning off the computer every night before bed. And while our paths will be different, if we really want it, quick financial freedom is within reach of us all.

Twelve Steps To Quick-Time Your Retirement

1. One Home, Not Two

Don't live alone, move in with someone. Live with your parents, your lover, your friend. When you get married, consider living with your parents or offering part of your house to a roommate. While cohabitation might be better for your mental health, the bottom line reason is that **sharing a home saves a lot of money**.

Let's say that you could save half the average mortgage, or about $600 a month, by sharing a house. If you invested that money in your 401(k), you'd also save on taxes. Assuming that you'd save about $250 on taxes for that $600 in the 401(k), you've just saved $250 + $600 = $850 every month. Whoa! If you take that $850 a month, and keep saving it at 6% interest (your goal is to beat inflation), it will be worth roughly $139,000 in ten years.

2. Don't Feed Your Ego

Drive a smaller car, keep it longer and get better gas mileage. If you drive two hundred-fifty miles a week in a fuel-efficient car, you could save half your gas money each month. And **never buy new**. You can save $100 a month right off the bat on a gently used car. Combine those two savings and you'll have $200 total to invest at 6%, giving you earnings of $32,700 over ten years. Really, do you need "big," "new," or "fancy," to feel good about yourself? No! You'll be feeling great knowing how much closer you are to financial freedom.

3. Take up Meditation (or Walking in the Woods)

It can be quite expensive to have bad habits, and very inexpensive to have good ones. Give up drugs, bad relationships, alcohol, overeating, cigarettes, *Cosmo* at the checkout (get it from the library if you must—but walk there), four beers with the boys, potato chips and recreational shopping. Instead go for walks, learn to meditate, take an inexpensive yoga class at a university, eat better, seek out supportive friendships and learn to window shop. You will save money on costs, medical bills and insurance premiums, while being in better shape physically and emotionally. The value of **changing these habits is priceless**: after all, what is your good health and happiness worth?

4. Say "No" to Expensive Insurance

Change deductibles on car insurance from $100 to $500 or $1,000. Change the deductible on your home to $1,000 or $2,500. Purchase term life insurance from Low Load or other companies listed in the insurance section. Drop life policies you don't need, leverage your group policies at work and use your medical reimbursement account if you have one.

Say "yes" to putting your savings in your IRA, 403(b), 401(k) or the qualified retirement plan. Each $100 saved monthly is worth $16,000 in ten years, $46,200 in twenty years, $100,000 in thirty years, $200,000 in forty years and $378,000 in fifty years, all at a 6% return. 6% over inflation is a good investment goal to ensure that the money you will have in the future will be equivalent to today's dollars.

Review Property and Liability Insurance issues at www.zenvesting.com

5. Say "Yes" to Frequent Flier Miles

Use your credit cards as much as you can for groceries, bills, clothing, car payments and so on. For every $20,000 to $40,000 in annual expense payments, you will have a "free" ticket or two per year. Of course, pay off the credit card each month and **never use credit cards for the credit**, only for the convenience and the frequent flier miles. In my family, we have an American Airlines card, which we use for business expenses; a Charles Schwab card, for personal expenses (which we can use on more than one airline); and a Northwest Airlines card, for rounding off miles we get for travel. Again, I stress that it's important to pay off the credit card balance each month. If you are not disciplined about budgeting, then credit cards for frequent flier miles, cash back, or convenience are not for you. In addition, be sure that everyone in your family, including children, has a frequent flyer account for each airline you fly.

6. Say "No" to Expensive Annuities, Load 12(b)1 and Back End Load Mutual Funds

If you save just 1% annually, it adds up fast—$1,000 monthly at 6% interest earns $693,000 in twenty-five years. At 7%, that would be $810,000, and at 8%, almost a $1,000,000. **That is real money!** So look at returns and expenses when investing. Use no load funds, and avoid expensive programs or Fund of Fund hedge funds.

7. Check 'Em Out

Don't hire anyone to help you manage your portfolio without thorough research. Never use anyone except an **experienced fee-only advisor** whose track record of investment success is at least ten years. Have them fill out the questionnaire at truthinperformance.com. Avoid the discount brokers' "free" services—a one size fits all "excellence" strategy doesn't exist.

8. Don't Be Reckless

Have good insurance with high limits, have a good umbrella policy, wear your seatbelt and helmet, **eat healthy, live healthy, maintain healthy relationships**, be honest, follow the law, live modestly, have a cash hoard, be prepared, have wills and trusts (if necessary) and investigate before funding any investment scheme. Someone heard the guy who fell off the Empire State Building say, "So far, so good," as he flew past the 17th floor! Other words of advice include: Drive a safe car, lock your doors at night, don't give out your personal information and protect your identity. Make sure that those you feel responsible for are not being stupid so you don't have to bail them out. For many retirees, bailing their children out of stupid mistakes messes up their retirements more than any other reason.

9. Don't Pay Down Your Home Mortgage

Don't pay down a home mortgage early unless you are fully funding your tax deductible 401(k), 403(b), IRA's, etc. Every $100 you pay down on your home is worth $446 in 25 years at 6% if you are in the 25% tax bracket. If, on the other hand, you put $100 more in your 401(k) and invest the tax savings of $25 or so, you will have, at 6%, $558 in 25 years. The bottom line is if you want to get out of debt faster, **accumulate your money in your retirement plans** and use that money to pay off your home in retirement. Even after taxes this makes sense because of the tax-free compounding and current tax savings. Your banker or mortgage person might disagree with this approach, so get a second opinion from a fee-only advisor.

10. Be Self Reliant

Take everything in this book with two bags of salt. Run it through your own common sense test. It should stand up to criticism and second and third opinions.

Another thought to ponder is that you should not expect a CPA to know about investing or a CFP® to know about taxes. If you want help with a global investment strategy, get that help from a global investment professional.

II. **Be Long Term**

Make your life great now. Relax and take a leisurely, long view of things. If you don't like what you see, get re-educated or re-skilled by going back to school. You Odeserve a career that you love. Get your life so wonderful that you never want to quit being who you are, and where you are.

I2. **Know Yourself**

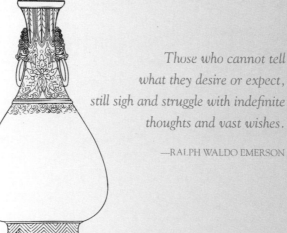

Those who cannot tell
what they desire or expect,
still sigh and struggle with indefinite
thoughts and vast wishes.

—RALPH WALDO EMERSON

WHAT MAKES PEOPLE DESPAIR
IS THAT THEY TRY TO FIND A
UNIVERSAL MEANING TO THE WHOLE
OF LIFE, AND THEN END UP BY
SAYING IT IS ABSURD, ILLOGICAL,
EMPTY OF MEANING. THERE IS NOT
ONE BIG COSMIC MEANING FOR ALL,
THERE IS ONLY THE MEANING
WE EACH GIVE TO OUR LIFE,
AN INDIVIDUAL MEANING,
AN INDIVIDUAL PLOT,
LIKE AN INDIVIDUAL NOVEL,
A BOOK FOR EACH PERSON.

—ANAÏS NIN

hapter 15

INVESTMENTS: CHICKENS, EGGS & NESTING STRATEGIES

*Middle age is when, given two choices, you choose
the one that gets you home by nine.* —RONALD REAGAN

When I was a child, my mother would kiss me on the forehead as she left to visit my grandmother saying, "Your grandma's seventy-six and she'll probably not make it to seventy-seven, so this might be the last time I'll get to see her." And each year she would drive the twelve-hour journey to a small coal-mining town in southeastern Ohio. This went on for twenty years!

Later, as a student in the investment business, I would listen to Mom remark upon how awful my uncle was because he would only allow Grandma her stock dividends and bond interest to live on, and would never let her spend the principle. Mom would say that Uncle Frank was too worried about inflation, and that he must be thinking that Grandma was going to live forever. Uncle Frank invested in stocks whose dividends tended to increase every few years, and remarkably, Grandma always had enough money each year to offset inflation. Well, Grandma lived to be ninety-six. "You know Paul," my mom said to me, "I used to argue with Uncle Frank about how he managed your Grandma's money as if she would live forever, but he was right."

When my grandmother died, Mom inherited her share of stocks and bonds, and I was amazed to see how well my uncle had chosen the securities for her portfolio. There were many different companies in industries that grew over the years, and most paid dividends. My uncle had carefully monitored Grandma's portfolio and managed for income growth and security. His efforts and willingness to stand up against my mom and not dip into the principle had been a great service to the whole family. Had they spent a portion of the principle when she was in her seventies, not only would Grandma have run out of money by the end of her life, she also would have had much less to spend after a few years.

Probable-Possible, my black hen,
She lays eggs in the Relative When.
She doesn't lay eggs in the Positive Now
Because she's unable to postulate how.
—FREDERICK ALBERT WINSOR

In 1973, the endowment trustees of Harvard University were confronted with rising costs, inflation, stagnant or diminishing government support and uncertain financial markets. They were determined to manage their assets in such a way as to assure perpetual, long-term security while stressing conservative spending policies, so they adopted a policy based upon the assumption that:

[
1. Inflation would average 4%.
2. The University's cost would increase 6% a year.
3. The endowment's total return would be around 8% with a portfolio of 65% in equities and 35% in bonds.
4. Gifts and bequests would average 2%.
]

The trustees decided to spend 4% of the endowment's market value annually. They based their annual spending target on the prevailing market value of assets, so that spending would not fluctuate based upon the "swinging" value of the portfolio. They also set up a stabilization fund to save excess earnings in good years to then be distributed in poor years.

Most investors bury their head in the sand when it comes to their investment portfolio. They neglect to look objectively at the inherent risks in their investments that should compel them to develop a risk minimization strategy. Unsuccessful investors scarcely acknowledge that investments do flounder for what seems like unexplainable reasons. Perhaps because of ease or convenience investors often use an oversimplified approach pushed by incompetent although often well meaning and honest brokers, bankers, CFPs, CPAs, lawyers and lucky friends. Nassin Nicholas Taleb, former Wall Street trader, now a scholar of the nuature of chance, says, "You can miss-predict everything for all your life yet think that you will get it right next time."

Other investors may wisely protect themselves from the aforementioned speculative investment sellers, but then ignore inflation. Inflation can be a devastating blow to your financial well-being by creeping up on a portfolio and slowly debilitating the investment's ability to provide a favorable income stream. A good rule of thumb is to never draw on your portfolio by more than 3% to 6% unless you are in dire need of the funds on a short-term basis. The long-term consequences of drawing from 3% to 6% may adversely affect your purchasing power, especially since we do not know the future. For portfolios that are actively managed under a strategy designed to avoid over-valued assets and favor their under-valued counterparts, 4% to 6% seems reasonable.

In retirement, what is important is paying a low price for a lot of income, but adjusting that decision with common sense and risk analysis. All investments have Bull and Bear Markets—markets are cyclical, just like the seasons. Stocks, bonds, real estate, gold, oil, art and antiques are all affected by investor psychology and mania cycles. The goal is to understand the importance of the following three concepts: buy low at bargain prices; sell when investments are expensive; and have patience.

Conceptually, you must look at your portfolio like a farmer views an egg-laying chicken. You wouldn't want to eat the chicken (your principle) nor would you want to eat all of the eggs (the income from your principle), because some of them will hatch into chicks that eventually lay more eggs (increasing the income to help offset inflation.)

Let's look at a scenario with two egg laying hens that each cost $5 five years ago. The first hen is an ordinary, one egg a day hen that now costs $10. The second hen is a beautiful, exquisite, rare, one-a-day egg-laying hen that has increased in price to $30 over the five years. Most folks would say, "You should buy the 'exotic' hen. Look how it performed in the past." Yet they are both egg-laying hens, and you eat eggs. So while the exquisite rare beauty of a hen is nice, a rational investor would say give me three of those ugly egg-layers for the price of one of the rare ones, because you can't eat beauty.

Do not let past performance of a specific investment guide your overall investing strategy. What it will produce in the future based on the price you pay is key. When people realize this, they will, if rational, sell their fancy hen to buy three ordinary ones—tripling their expected future returns and reducing the risk that the fancy hen might stare at herself in a pond and starve to death.

chapter 16

INVESTING:
IT'S ABOUT LUCK

Never expose yourself unnecessarily to danger; a miracle may not save
you…and if it does, it will be deducted from your share of luck or merit.
—THE TALMUD

Over my life I have met many successful people and have invested in many successful companies—I now truly believe that success is all about "luck." **Pure luck.** Successful people were lucky because they chose to take responsibility and behave in a way that allowed luck to happen. They were lucky because they saved money so they could invest it. They were lucky because they educated themselves on investing basics and wisely chose the right path for their portfolio so it could grow. They diversified their investments wisely to increase their chance of being lucky.

My goal is to make it so you can be a lucky investor. I've spent my adult life managing money and we at FIM Group have generally been lucky most of those years. And, of course, we have periods when we have felt just plain unlucky, like 2008. When we felt that wind energy could be successful, we were lucky because we studied the industry and the companies in that industry and spent time in analysis to find the ones that were real and had good management, good products and solid financing. We were lucky because we bought the shares when they were bargain priced and sold them for a gain. These in turn were bought not by investors but by speculators who had no idea if they should pay $50 or $10 a share for the wind energy companies. Were we lucky when shares became bargained priced once more and we bought shares again? Yes, because we acted on knowledge and experience and with the discipline to allow our investments funds to compound.

So What Do Lucky Investors Do?

1st)   They save so that they have money to invest
2nd)   They understand the power of compounding
3rd)   They understand that investments are tools
4th)   They learn that everything is cyclical, connected, dynamic, and that when investments become expensive they should be sold; when they are bargains, they should be bought
5th)   They learn about investing concepts or they delegate and hire someone to help them

Go to www.zenvesting.com for more investing resources.

People always call it luck when you've acted more sensibly than they have.

—ANNE TYLER

I'm a great believer in luck,
and I find the harder I work the more I have of it.—THOMAS JEFFERSON

Here, I'm going to concentrate on helping you delegate this important function by using good mutual funds or an investment manager. As president of FIM Group I manage with my team: portfolios for individuals, families, trusts, foundations and retirement plans. I've spent twenty-five years managing portfolios and have strong opinions on how money should be managed and like everything in this book my words should meet your common sense test. Naturally, you should read the prospectus (and other information) on any investment before you invest your money.

Finding a money manager or fund that is just "lucky" is really not how you want to invest. How do you know if your investment manager is skilled, disciplined and destined to be lucky long term? Simple: remember seven years + three times. A money manager with a ten-year track record has three seven-year periods to look at to see if they have skill. Scientific analysis shows that with anything less than seven to ten years—even if they've had what look to be huge, unbelievably lucky results—there's no accurate forecast of the future.

The Evaluation Letter on page 190 comes from www.zenvesting.com and should be mailed to any company you're thinking of hiring. Remember to trust your intuition and ask for the references of the advisor.

Ethical and Sustainable Investing

I've been investing since 1973 and have thought a great deal about sustainable and ethical investments. I feel that the bottom line is that I want to invest at the right price in sustainable investments that help people live healthy happy lives. I don't want to put money in products that kill or exploit people. I don't want to contribute, through my dollar, to corruption, indifference, waste and poison. I care about people, the environment, our interconnected world.

Avoiding investment managers that use indexes or value-neutral passive benchmarked strategies can help you steer clear of exchange-traded funds (ETF) or companies that you may feel fall into these categories of wasteful, harmful or exploitative.

As I mentioned earlier, to be a successful investor **knowledge and skill are the key to being lucky and creating a successful sustainable portfolio.**

Practical Help

I would love to say go to a discount broker, or registered fee-only advisor and take their advice, but I can't. The world is too dynamic and companies seem to get stuck in selling what will sell rather than what is right for investors long term. However a good start if you want to get help is to find a fee-only advisor with at least ten years experience. Then sit down with them and go over your professional checklist.

The list of discount brokers at www.zenvesting.com are good starting points for investing.

A professional checklist can be found at www.zenvesting.com in the Investing section.

There is no such thing as luck.
There is only adequate or inadequate
preparation to cope with a statistical universe.
—ROBERT HEINLEIN

A wealth of information to guide you with investing, buying insurance, financial, estate planning and retirement planning is available at www.zenvesting.com.

- Glossary of Financial & Investment Terms
- Complete listing of Discount Brokers
- Links to great websites that will help you gain knowledge about investing, economics, retirement, travel, budgeting and more.
- Financial Periodicals and their websites
- Sample Retirement Investment Policies & Strategies

It is practical to set up an account with a discount broker to "hold" your money. I will admit a favorable "personal and business bias" toward discount brokers. I think most firms are honest, caring people that want to help investors and of course they also want grow their share value and sell what sells. **All discount brokers must be looked at like a grocery store.** They are happy to profit from selling you cigarettes, rot gut food or alcohol, and equally happy selling you organic locally grown tomatoes. Another problem is that the sales pitch may sound organic, but is really only green-washing. Be on your guard—investigate before you invest.

Most discount brokers will allow you to set up a management account that can collect your deposits and allow you to invest in thousands of no load mutual funds. The account can issue a checkbook and most offer twenty-four hour phone support, online support and low costs.

What helps luck is a habit of watching for opportunities,
of having a patient, but restless mind,
of sacrificing one's ease or vanity,
of uniting a love of detail to foresight, and of
passing through hard times bravely and cheerfully.

—CHARLES VICTOR CHERBULIEZ

*Toldos Yaakov Yosef offers an
allegorical rendering. In order
to ascend a mountain, one must
free himself of excess baggage
and bulky clothing so that he
may travel as lightly as possible.
This is doubly true in the attempt
to scale spiritual heights. One
who is unencumbered by the
weight of possessions and social
commitments can be light [in
order to] rise to the top.*

—MOSHE LIEBER, *THE PIRKEI AVOS
TREASURY: ETHICS OF THE FATHERS*

hapter 17

ESTATE PLANNING

The world is too much with us; late and soon
Getting and spending, we lay waste our powers…
—WILLIAM WORDSWORTH

In the course of a long and full life, we usually acquire assets that can be thought of as a gift to be passed on to family, charity, society or friends. The amazing thing about estate planning is that it only benefits someone else, truly making it compassionate and unusually spiritual at its very core. But this act of benevolence requires a bit more forethought than you might expect. Estate planning means that you assign title to your assets—a court of law will decide ownership if you don't. The title determines what happens to the assets in the event of your death. **Ultimately, you can't die without a plan—either you have one designed based on your own intentions and values or one is decided for you by the blind, cold legal system.**

A typical estate consists of some, or all, of the following assets: home, other real estate, furnishings and personal property, vehicles and recreational equipment, antiques and collectibles, cash, checking and savings accounts, stocks and bonds, life insurance, retirement plans, mortgages and land contracts.

Each of these items—if owned by you—comprises your estate. If they are owned jointly, they are still part of your estate for tax purposes, but not for probate purposes.

In approaching an intentional estate plan there are some general questions to answer:

- What are the elements of your estate (assets, insurance, loans, etc.) and who owns them?

- What are your objectives and intentions? Most people want to leave money to family members, to help friends, to give to charity, to start a foundation and to provide security for your children and family.

- Who will help you set up your plan?

- Which of the available tools (wills, trusts, life insurance, joint ownership, etc.) will best accomplish your objectives? Your advisors can help you with this.

- Who is responsible for keeping your estate plan current?

Courage means being well aware of the worst that can happen,
being scared almost to death, and then doing the right thing anyhow.
—WILLIAM SLOANE COFFIN

The first step in preparing your estate plan is to make a list of what you own, their values and how they are owned. This can be done with the help of an asset schedule and serves as the starting point of an estate planning discussion with your advisors. Think of it as a permanent inventory of your estate that can be updated and reviewed as it changes.

After you have made your list, you must decide your objectives; several popular ones are listed below:

- Creating and conserving the estate for the benefit of your family, charity, business interests or friends.

- Providing for the orderly disposition of assets.

- Reducing taxes and costs.

- Arranging for the management of your estate by a competent personal representative or trustee.

- Leaving a legacy to friends, family, charity, society, church or foundation.

There is an Estate Asset and Value Schedule Worksheet on page 189.

Finally, you need to be intentional about who you designate as your beneficiaries and what you want to leave them. Any changes in your estate or family situation may require changes in your present plan. Again, if you do not have a will, trust or other estate planning documents, state law determines who will receive the assets. Since this law is inflexible and written to apply to general situations, it does not take into consideration any special circumstances involving your estate and/or family situation. It is vitally important to avoid having the state decide questions of estate. Estate planning is a critical element of good financial planning; being aware and responsible ensures your future wishes.

Once you have determined what you have in your estate and your plan for those assets, you can then decide upon the available estate planning tools that might best accomplish your wishes.

Be grateful to institutions that have helped you, not just individuals.
The Midrash teaches: "A person must be grateful to a
place where he derived some benefit." (Genesis Rabbah 79:6)

—RABBI JOSEPH TELUSHKIN IN *A CODE OF JEWISH ETHICS*

Wills, Trusts & Other Estate Planning Tools

A will is a document that contains directions for the management and disposition of your estate following your death. It is administrated through Probate Court and so it must be prepared according to applicable state law. A will does not enable a person to avoid probate, but enables a person to set forth their wishes as to how the estate will be probated, and to whom and when that estate will be distributed. Probate is the process that ensures that the wishes expressed in the will are carried out. The act of having a will prepared for you (and signing it) means you won't be restricted—during your lifetime—from changing the ownership, administration, or disposition of any of the assets that you own. Your will, though valid if prepared according to applicable state law, isn't effective until you die.

A trust is a separate legal entity created by means of a trust document, either separately or as a part of your will. The trust may be in the form of a "testamentary" trust that is included as part of your will, and comes into existence following your death and after the probate of your estate. Trusts may also take the form of a living trust, sometimes referred to as a revocable living (or loving) trust, which is a separate document from your will and is funded during your lifetime.

The revocable living trust is entirely revocable during your lifetime, to the extent that it is funded with your assets during your lifetime. The assets in the trust will not be probated at the time of your death because the trust is a separate legal entity and its existence continues after your death. A living trust allows you control over the trust assets and administration; you can name yourself as trustee and administer the trust assets during your lifetime, with a successor trustee named in the document to take over the administration of the trust assets immediately upon your death.

The trust can also be used to reduce estate taxes by dividing your estate following your death into separate shares for surviving spouse, children, friends, family and marital trusts.

The trust, whether a living trust or a testamentary trust, may also be designed simply for the purpose of receiving insurance proceeds following your death. In addition, it might contain the directions for administration and distribution of those proceeds, with no other assets intended as trust funding.

An irrevocable trust may be appropriate if one of your objectives is to remove assets from your estate for the benefit of other beneficiaries without an immediate outright distribution to those beneficiaries.

You may also accomplish estate reduction by means of gifts. If these annual gifts are less than $12,000 per person, they will not incur a gift tax. If the gifts are to charitable, religious, educational or similar organizations, they may qualify for the income tax charitable deduction. Such trusts are not usually subject to an amount limitation. Also, 529 college plan contributions have estate tax benefits.

The Durable Power of Attorney is another important estate planning tool. This is a document wherein you designate someone as your "attorney-in-fact" and give them limited or broad powers to handle your business affairs, including making personal decisions for you in the event that you become incompetent. It is valid only during your lifetime; any such authority granted in that document terminates upon your death. It can allow you to avoid the involvement of a probate court in the establishment of a guardianship or conservatorship to supervise the administration of your estate or personal decisions during any period in which you are unable to make decisions for yourself for either mental or physical reasons.

Act without striving.
Work without interfering.
Find the flavour in what is flavourless.
Enlarge the small, increase the few.
Heal injury with goodness.
Handle the difficult while it is still easy.
Cultivate the great while it is still small.
All difficult things begin as easy things.
All great things begin as small things.
Therefore, the True Person never attempts anything great,
and accomplishes great things.
Lightly made promises inspire little faith.
Trying to make things easy results in great difficulties.
Therefore, the True Person regards everything as difficult,
and is never overcome by difficulties.

—TAO TE CHING

Preparing People

In addition to preparing for death in legal terms, prepare your loved ones emotionally. Write a letter to key players outlining your wishes, and how they are to be carried out. The argument exists that estate planning is a grand preparation for something that—least of all—benefits the planner, so why do it at all? Life and love are also about preparation.

- Your spouse (or father, mother, siblings, children, friends, etc.) should know who to call if you die, and where to find a list of your assets and important papers.

- Prepare a letter that includes a list of people you believe can be trusted as advisors for accounting, legal work, investment advice, insurance and general financial planning help.

- Your spouse and adult children should know or have a letter about your specific wishes concerning funeral details, including cremation, burial, organ gifting and cemetery choice.

- Your children should know whom you have named as guardians and why you chose those particular people.

After a life of magnificent pleasures and stunning heartbreaks, death does seem a bit anticlimactic. You will be remembered by how you positively or negatively influenced the people around you. What do you want your legacy to be?

A Few Words on Choice of Guardians

For a couple with children, the most important estate planning decision is naming a guardian in case of death. This can be a very difficult decision. Ideally, you want a stable couple who shares your values and loves your children as much as you do. Your family or friends perhaps have already built relationships with your children, and you have been able to watch them parent their own children. In this way you can get a feel for their philosophy and values. Once you have made a selection, it is entirely appropriate for you to sit down and ask them if they would be willing to be named guardians of your children.

After you have chosen your guardians, give them detailed instructions regarding how you want the children raised in the event of your death. This should include subjects ranging from education, religion and discipline, to your philosophy on spiritual matters and family responsibilities.

Usually it is best to have your guardians separate from matters of assets, investments and insurance money. It's preferable to have separate trustees handle the money so that your guardians—who may be the world's greatest parents and the world's worst money managers—have no perceived conflicts of interest. The trustee simply makes a check payable to the guardians every month for the support, maintenance, health and education of your children.

Also, for our children, the trustees were instructed to look at the guardian situation from an "all-is-one" point of view. Amy and I don't want our children to have private school if the guardian's children are going to public school, and we don't want our kids to have a closet full of new clothes while their own children are dressed in hand-me-downs. The trustees would have a lump sum come in monthly for the guardians to throw into the family budget, and would be instructed not to earmark it "For My Kids Alone."

Sadly, I find that people often spend more time figuring out what type of life insurance to purchase or which lawyer to use to draw up their estate plan, than in making the critical decision of who they'll choose as the guardians of their children and how they would want their assets used to benefit those they love. The bottom line of all this estate planning is to reflect your love and compassion beyond your death.

What Legacy Do You Wish to Leave?

I remember being involved in a family meeting with a client's children to disclose that upon their parents' death, each of them would inherit enough money to significantly change their financial lives. The parents' goal at the family meeting was to tell their kids to relax, and to quit worrying about retirement and saving for the education of their children, because they would inherit enough to provide for those two needs.

Imagine the complex thoughts of the children. I'm sure they ranged from difficulty accepting the inevitable death of their parents to relief that their future financial needs would be taken care of. One of the daughters said, "For the past few months I've been losing sleep over whether to set aside $25 a week for retirement or send Cassidy to singing lessons."

Another daughter remarked, "My gosh, I've been wrestling with working more and putting the kids in an after-school latch key arrangement so that we can save for a college fund. I'd love to quit my second job so that I could be home when they get off the bus." The grateful daughter's eyes then filled with tears, and hugs abounded.

Finally, we talked about the portion of the estate that would be taxed at 66% unless the children all agreed to give it to a charity instead. The parents purposely opted out of this conversation, but were proud to see their offspring excitedly spending two hours discussing a long list of social ills they might possibly influence with a donation from their parents' estate.

Here's where you need to segue into a legacy and what that means to you, and to someone else. What are your values? If you die with $50 in your pocket or $50 million in assets, what legacy do you wish to leave? It is a tragedy that so many estate plans represent the neutral values of the attorney drafting the wills and trusts, with not nearly enough thoughtful input from you, their client.

See the My Way/Our Way Legacy Plan, downloadable online at www.zenvesting.com.

Event-Driven Dispositions

If you knew that in five years you were going to receive $1 million, would it change your behavior now? Would your life be different if, when you turned eighteen, someone told you that you would receive $500,000 on your twenty-fifth birthday, $500,000 at thirty, and $1 million at thirty-five? In all probability, you would not be in the position you are in today. I don't believe maturity comes with age necessarily, yet people still set up age-driven dispositions in their trust. The result? Kids biding their time, with no particular ambition, because they know they'll receive the jackpot just by getting older. Go watch old folks putting coins in slot machines for entertainment—is that what you would want your kids doing?

A more conscious and individualized way of distributing assets to heirs is under what I call "event-driven dispositions." Rather than leaving a lump sum, you might, for example, set up a trust to pay for all of your children's college expenses and provide them with a $200 monthly stipend for food, books, travel, and extra expenses. Include a cash settlement when they graduate as a big carrot.

You could also structure the disposition so that your children get equal portions of your estate when they graduate, earn a post-doctorate degree, have a child, marry, buy their first home, start a business and complete a stint in missionary-type work or the Peace Corps. Some documents simply allow the trustee to match the earned income of the beneficiary. Most estate attorneys are entirely familiar with event-driven dispositions and will generally try to work with you to have an individual, custom and creative estate plan.

Other interesting ideas I have seen in trusts include having the children direct a certain amount of money to a charity each month; providing funds for travel, often exotic, for the family to meet for an annual gathering; and releasing a lump sum for traveling the world or for taking a special trip to a specific destination.

I grew up among the Sages.
All my life I listened to their words.
Yet I have found nothing better than silence.
Study is not the goal, doing is.
Do not mistake "talk" for "action."
Pity fills no stomach.
Compassion builds no house.
Understanding is not yet justice.
Whoever multiplies words causes confusion.
The truth that can be spoken
Is not the Ultimate Truth.
Ultimate Truth is wordless,
the silence within the silence.
More than the absence of speech,
More than the absence of words,
Ultimate Truth is the seamless being-in-place
that comes with attending to Reality.
—SHIMON BEN GAMLIEL

hapter 18

CONCLUSION

So now we come to the end of this book and I will consider your journey a success if you say, "I can."

I can figure out what I want . . .

I can figure out what I don't want . . .

I can find my priorities . . .

I can establish commitments . . .

I can say "no" to unhealthy habits . . .

I can set goals . . .

I can have it all . . . by establishing what I really want the "all" to look like . . .

I can choose to be kind . . .

I can choose to be compassionate . . .

I can be responsible . . .

When life throws me a zinger, I can say "Oh good, an opportunity to grow, learn, accept and love."

I can be prepared for a Katrina or a snowstorm . . .

Of course all this "I can" stuff takes courage—it might take courage by the bucketful. Saying "I can" and "Oh good!" empowers you. They are the opposite of "can't." "Can't" is a word more vile than any swear word. It keeps our songs unsung, our dreams unfulfilled, our intentions powerless and our inner voices mute. Ultimately, good intentions don't influence the living of a beautiful healthy, successful, happy life: only actions do. So get rid of "can't" and say "I can and I will."

I will get a will.

I will fund my 401(k).

I will write "thank-you" notes.

I will choose to smile.

I will take responsibility for my actions, my life and my thoughts.

I will adopt healthy habits.

I will walk more.

I will throw "victim" out of my body, mind, emotions and vocabulary.

I will get a budget and live within my means.

I will enhance my education.

I will work harder, better, happier and more pleasantly at work.

I will say "Hi, how are you?"

I will thank my lover for loving me.

I will thank my children for choosing me as their parent.

I will appreciate my parents, despite any childhood scars.

I will give up judging good or bad and embrace acceptance.

I will concentrate on right behavior.

Inertia is our hindrance to action, ego helps support our bad habits, others might resist our changes and some may tease us about our positive attitude. The reason so many successful, enthusiastically happy people are loners is because well-meaning friends give support only by offering the cold water word "can't." If my son wants to play for Manchester United someday, he can! Why should anyone think they are helping him or supporting him by using the word "can't"? I would rather say, "If you work hard, train often, and are dedicated, Manchester United might just take you on."

> *If you do follow your bliss, you put yourself on a kind of track*
> *that had been there all the while, waiting for you, and the life*
> *you ought to be living is the one you are living.* —JOSEPH CAMPBELL

Christian, Jewish, Buddhist and Muslim religions all value love and acceptance, as well as an element of awe. They embrace the extraordinary idea that miracles do happen—that anything is possible in our lives if we do not fear life. Do you express love to yourself; do you embrace life's possibilities with innocence and courage? You are your own best friend, but do you treat yourself with respect? Or do you express your fear instead, avoiding life through laziness, inertia, excuses, victim hood and negativity? Love or fear—it's your choice!

If I act with kindness, then my action is kindness. The sincerity of our actions and our good intentions are "reason" enough for doing the right thing. To create healthy habits we need to re-program backwards from each act. Express the acts you think are right. Don't intellectualize this, be Taoist: don't think too much, trust nature, trust your higher, loving, balanced, natural self to guide your spontaneous, right actions.

The Zen of Abundance

If we are to grow in our awareness of the global economic reality, it is necessary for all compassionate Zen students to expand their financial understanding beyond a personal level.

Look at healthy communities. They are either a democracy or ruled by an enlightened leadership who encourages creativity and communication. People are productive and happiest when involved in work and relationships that benefit the community. Economics is the fundamental reality of their relationships.

Envy, greed and laziness are the three archenemies of both community and individuals. They are abundance restrictors, hampering individuals from pursuing beneficial relationships. Societies work if people are responsible. The wise leader says to the lazy: please work. To the greedy: please share. To the envious: go away if you are unwilling to cooperate.

A Zen Master in his late nineties fell ill and bedridden. He refused to eat, citing the explanation, "In our community, to eat today, you must work today." His students pleaded with him, "Master, we will share. Please eat." To which the Master replied, "To eat today, work today."

The students were unable to persuade him until they finally lifted the Master's bed and placed it in the garden, tossing out the scarecrow. Productive again, the Master spent his last days throwing rocks at crows and munching on juicy tomatoes fresh off the vine.

The bountiful river of life demands work and balance. Our personal success in living in the real economic world is no matter of luck and happenstance. Right effort, engaging skills and the production of something useful leads to happiness, financial success and a healthy community.

My closing wish for you:

As I breathe and smile throughout my day, I will serve others, I will be aware of the needs of others, including all people, all animals, our living earth and all sentient beings. I am conscious of the changes I want in the world. I will be conscious that all individuals are working out their own paths. Envy, judgment, jealousy and intolerance must not cloud my desire to love and serve. I realize that peace must begin with me and be within me, so I will treat my body, mind and spirit with respect. I will allow myself and others to change. I know that today I have the power of choice and can decide to embrace that which brings harmony, love, prosperity and joy to my world.

If you choose, you can do it, too. Now take this book and implement its guidance. I know you can, I know you can. I hope you realize every dream you can dream.

Sincerely,

Paul

Paul Sutherland

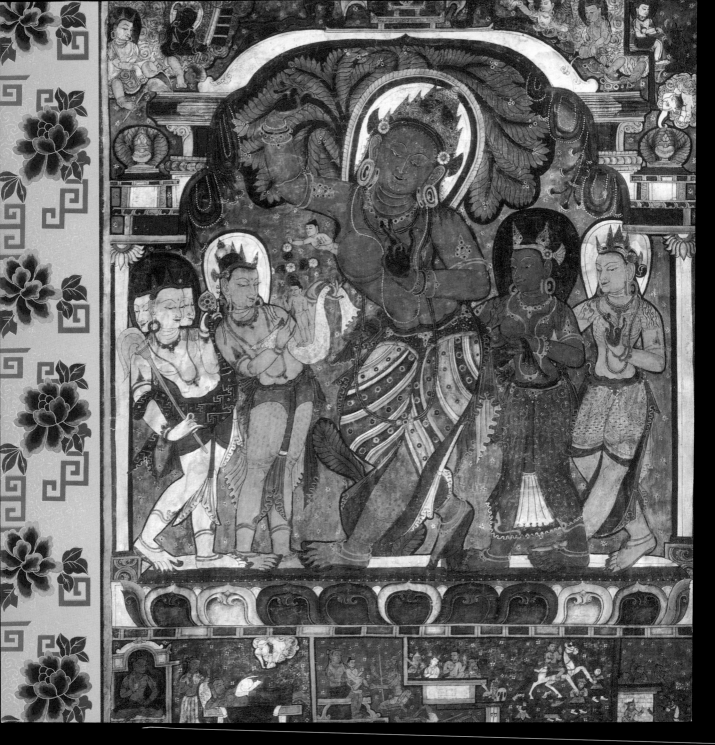

GENTLE BUDGETING WORKSHEET

	Month 1	Month 2	Month 3	Average
INCOME (Total for month)				
EXPENSES				
Mortgage/Rent				
Property Taxes				
Car Payments				
Auto Expenses				
Phone *(personal)*				
Electricity & Heating				
Home Maintenance				
Food				
Child Care				
Entertainment				
Holiday				
Sanity *(yoga, counseling)*				
Fun *(wine, cigars, latte)*				
Personal Development & Education				
Helping Others				
Tithing				
Insurance *(home, health, life)*				
2nd Home				
Net Investment Expenses				
Credit Cards *(maintenance charges or payments on debt)*				
Other				
TOTAL EXPENSES				
Subtract **TOTAL EXPENSES** from **INCOME**				

INSURANCE CHECKLIST

You should review your insurance coverage amount regularly every twelve to eighteen months. You should also review

- if you get married

- the day you or your spouse becomes pregnant

- if someone becomes dependent on you, like a parent, sibling or child

- if your debt structure changes; if you take on new dept or pay off an old one

- if you net worth increases by $25,000 or more

- if you change jobs, take on a business partner, or change business forms (incorporate)

INSURANCE FOR LIFE WORKSHEET

STEP 1

On the lines below, list the names of the people who would suffer financially if you died. Beside their names, list what type of loss they would suffer—income, debt payback, family care, etc.

_____

_____

_____

STEP 2

Here, be specific about how much each of these people need.

_____ needs a monthly income of $ _____

_____ needs a monthly income of $ _____

_____ needs a monthly income of $ _____

_____ Pay of debts of $ _____ for _____ to_____

_____ Pay of debts of $ _____ for _____ to_____

_____ Pay of debts of $ _____ for _____ to_____

_____ needs a cash resource to be held in the amount of $ _____

_____ needs a cash resource to be held in the amount of $ _____

_____ needs a lump sum of special cash in the amount of $ _____

_____ needs a lump sum of special cash in the amount of $ _____

STEP 3

Add up the total monthly incomes from above ($___) and divide by .005 what is this for $___

Add up the total amount of money needed to pay off debts, mortgages, cash resources and special cash. $___

A. Here, you'll calculate the total amount of assets needed to provide for the above. ??

B. Now, make a list of all the liquid assets you own, or assets that could be made liquid, like X X X; calculate their value and put the total here: $___

Subtract liquid assets (B) from the assets needed (A) $___

This is the total insurance death benefit you will need to purchase.

KEY DISABILITY INCOME INSURANCE PROVISIONS

Your Disability Income Insurance Policy is the most important insurance you can own. Make sure you policy fits your needs completely, and without loopholes.

Here are some key provisions you should look for:

What you want : and Why

1. **Pays out at age 65 or a Lifetime benefit, if possible:** To provide for your long term security, want your insurance to pay you until at least age 65.

2. **A favorable definition of "disability," regarding either A) Your Occupation, or B) With Residual:** A **Your Occupation** definition protects your ability to earn a living doing whatever you do now. This kind of policy will pay you even if you end up working in another profession. A **With Residual** provides a benefit tied either to earnings lost or the percent of time spent at an occupation that was lost due to a disability. A benefit based on your earnings is far superior to one that's based on time lost, and should always be purchased. In fact, and "earnings lost" residual is better that a **Your Occupation** policy. Some of these "earnings lost" policies will pay full benefits even if you're earning 49% of your pre-disability pay.

3. **A Cost of Living / Inflation Protection benefit:** Having a policy that stays in step with price increases, or inflation, is very important. The minimum increase you should consider purchasing is 6% a year, and up to three times the policy benefit (a current benefit of $4000 a month for example, could raise to a $12,000 a month maximum). Just so you know, there are some policies that increase benefits over time, regardless of inflation.

4. **Non-cancelable and guaranteed renewable coverage:** What this means is that the policy can't be changed by anyone but yourself. It also means that premiums are guaranteed to increase above the level stated in the original policy.

5. **A Subsequent Disability Reoccurrence provision:** If you become disabled again from the same or another cause, this provision will waive a new elimination period.

6. **The earnings definition should include pension contributions and all bonuses:** This will assure that you receive your residual benefits.

7. **Make sure that pre-existing conditions are covered if they're listed on the policy application:** Some policies only cover sicknesses or accidents that manifest while the policy is in force. Claims on old high school back troubles could be denied if your policy doesn't cover disclosed, pre-existing conditions.

DISABILITY INCOME INSURANCE WORKSHEET

To calculate how much money you'll need to support yourself and your family in case of an illness or accident,

A) Write down the total of your average monthly expenses $ _____

Now, list the current investments you could quickly convert to cash

_____
_____
_____
_____
_____
_____
_____
_____
_____
_____

B) Add up the worth of these investments $ _____

Divide that amount (B) by your necessary monthly income (A) ____
That number equals the number of months your personal funds will support you.

ESTATE ASSETS AND VALUE SCHEDULE

There are various objectives in estate planning. You may wish to benefit family or friends. You may wish to make the disposition of your assets as unstressful as possible for your beneficiaries after your gone. You may simply wish to reduce taxes and court costs. Any or all of these will be served by determining the value of your estate.

Item	Market Value	Original Cost	Location	Ownership

EVALUATION LETTER TO AN ACCOUNT BROKER

Dear (name of broker):

I am considering setting up an account with your company, and will use predominantly open– and closed-end mutual funds to construct my portfolio. Will you allow me to buy no-load mutual funds? (Please send me a list of those funds.)

- What load mutual funds will you hold in my account on my behalf, if I already own some?
- Can I buy individually listed stocks? Bonds? Cds, et cetera?
- What money market fund do you automatically invest my cash balance in?
- Do you have no-transaction-fee funds (NTF)? If so, please send me details.

Please send me a letter addressing the above questions. In addition, I would also like to have verification that you are a member of the Securities Investors Protection Corporation, as well as of the Stock Exchange and thus regulated by their rules and regulations. Also, please send me your corporation's latest annual and quarterly reports. I'd like to receive these reports on a regular basis so that I can monitor your company's financial success. Additionally, would you outline your confidentiality safeguards and state that you will not sell my name to anyone for any reason.

In your new investor packet, please include the following:

1. A commission schedule so that I can get an accurate idea of what it will cost me to transact business through your company.

2. The name of a contact person that I may call to get more information.

3. A sample copy of your monthly portfolio statements. Will you list all my mutual funds on my monthly statements in addition to my other assets?

You should also know that I am interesting in establishing a relationship with you only if you will hold all of my assets in one street name or master account.

Finally, will your company issue me check-writing privileges on my non-retirement account? Can you issue a VISA debit card? What are the costs of each of these?

Thank you for your earliest attention to the above.

Sincerely,
(prospective account holder)

INDEX